Computers Simplified

— 2nd Edition —

VISUAL  SERIES

by: maranGraphics' Development Group

Corporate Sales

Contact maranGraphics
Phone: (905) 890-3300, ext.206
     (800) 469-6616, ext.206
Fax: (905) 890-9434

Canadian Trade Sales

Contact Prentice Hall Canada
Phone: (416) 293-3621
     (800) 567-3800
Fax: (416) 299-2529

Computers Simplified, 2nd Edition

Copyright©   1995 by maranGraphics Inc.
                5755 Coopers Avenue
                Mississauga, Ontario, Canada
                L4Z 1R9

Screen shots reprinted with permission from Microsoft Corporation.
WordPerfect 6.1 for Windows screen shots, © 1991, 1994 Novell, Inc. All Rights Reserved. Used with permission.
Screen shots/Picture from PerfectOffice 3.0 Standard 1994. Novell, Inc. All Rights Reserved. Used with permission.
Screen shots ©1995 Lotus Development Corporation. Used with permission of Lotus Development Corporation.
Screen shots for the Internet section reprinted with permission from Internet Direct ™.
Sierra On-Line, Inc. screen shots © Sierra On-Line, Inc., and used with permission.
Mavis Beacon Typing! is a registered trademark of Mindscape, Inc. screen shot used with permission.
Microsoft (R) Dinosaurs (c) & (p) 1993 Microsoft Corporation with images from Dorling Kindersley.
Microsoft (R) Musical Instruments (c) & (p) 1993 Microsoft Corporation with images from Dorling Kindersley.
Microsoft (R) Encarta TM (c) 1992-1994 Microsoft Corporation and Funk and Wagnalls Corporation.
Golf (c) 1994 Microsoft Corporation.

Canadian Cataloguing in Publication Data
Maran, Ruth, 1970-
          Computers simplified
(Visual 3-D series)
2nd ed.
Written by Ruth Maran.
First ed. published under title: MaranGraphics computers simplified / Richard Maran, Eric Feistmantl.
ISBN 1-896283-05-5
1. Microcomputers. I. maranGraphics' Development Group. II. Maran, Richard. MaranGraphics' computers simplified. III. Title. IV. Series.
QA76.5.M2268 1995   004.16   C95-931260-9

Printed in the United States of America

10   9   8   7   6   5   4   3   2

Trademark Acknowledgments

maranGraphics Inc. has attempted to include trademark information for products, services and companies referred to in this guide. Although maranGraphics Inc. has made reasonable efforts in gathering this information, it cannot guarantee its accuracy.

Dell® is a registered trademark of Dell Computer Corporation.

Intel and Pentium are registered trademarks and OverDrive is a trademark of Intel Corporation.

NetWare and WordPerfect are registered trademarks and GroupWise and PerfectOffice are trademarks of Novell, Inc.

Lotus, 1-2-3 and SmartSuite are registered trademarks of Lotus Development Corporation.

All other brand names and product names used in this book are trademarks, registered trademarks, or trade names of their respective holders. maranGraphics Inc. is not associated with any product or vendor mentioned in this book.

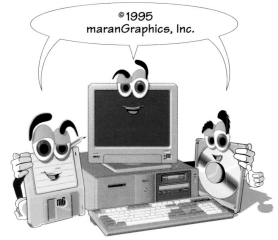

The animated characters are the copyright of maranGraphics, Inc.

Computers Simplified

—— 2nd Edition ——

maranGraphics™

Credits

Author and Architect:
Ruth Maran

Technical Consultant:
Geof Wheelwright

Layout Artist:
Christie Van Duin

Illustrations:

Dave Ross
David de Haas
Tamara Poliquin
Chris K.C. Leung
Carol Walthers
Suzanna Pereira

Editors:
Judy Maran
Kelleigh Wing

Proofreaders:

Paul Lofthouse
Brad Hilderley

Indexer:
Mark Kmetzko

Post Production:
Robert Maran

Acknowledgments

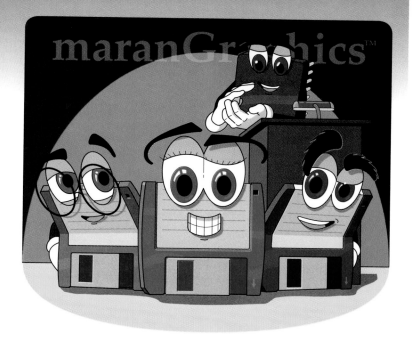

Thanks to the dedicated staff of maranGraphics, including
Maria Bellefleur, David de Haas, Brad Hilderley, Chris K.C.
Leung, Paul Lofthouse, Judy Maran, Maxine Maran, Robert Maran,
Sherry Maran, Tamara Poliquin, Dave Ross, Christie Van Duin,
Carol Walthers and Kelleigh Wing. Thanks also to Peters Ezers.

Finally, to Richard Maran who originated the easy-to-use graphic
format of this guide. Thank you for your inspiration and guidance.

TABLE OF CONTENTS

GETTING STARTED

THE BASIC COMPUTER

INPUT AND OUTPUT

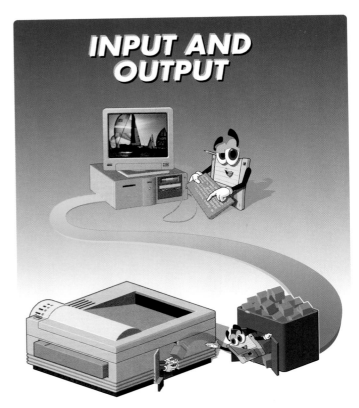

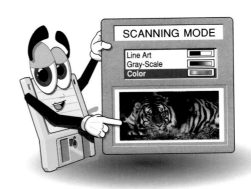

PROCESSING

MULTIMEDIA

STORAGE

TABLE OF CONTENTS

PORTABLE COMPUTERS

OPERATING SYSTEMS

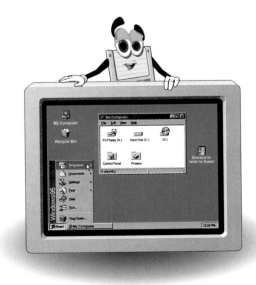

APPLICATION SOFTWARE

NETWORKS

In this chapter you will learn the difference between computer hardware and software. You will also learn about the main functions of a computer system.

GETTING STARTED

Hardware and Software

How Computers Work

HARDWARE AND SOFTWARE

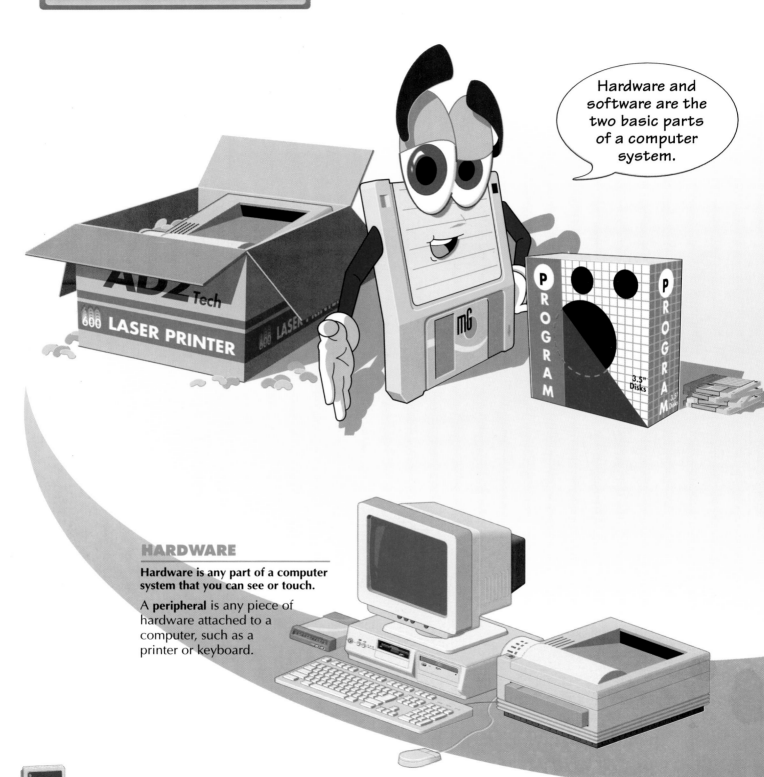

Hardware and software are the two basic parts of a computer system.

HARDWARE

Hardware is any part of a computer system that you can see or touch.

A **peripheral** is any piece of hardware attached to a computer, such as a printer or keyboard.

4

SOFTWARE

Software is a set of electronic instructions that tell the computer what to do. You cannot see or touch software, although you can see the packaging it comes in. Without software, computer hardware is like an airplane without a pilot.

You generally use floppy disks to load software onto your computer. You can also use a CD-ROM disc to load some software. This is a much faster method.

Note: If your computer is part of a network, you can load software by transferring the data through the network.

TYPES OF SOFTWARE

Application Software

Application software lets you accomplish specific tasks. You can use application software to write letters, analyze numbers, sort files, manage finances, draw pictures and even play games.

Some popular application software includes WordPerfect, Lotus 1-2-3 and Microsoft Access.

Operating System Software

Operating system software sets the rules for how computer hardware and application software work together.

The most popular operating system software includes MS-DOS and Windows.

5

HOW COMPUTERS WORK

A computer collects, processes, outputs and stores information.

INFORMATION

INPUT

Input devices provide a way of communicating with a computer. These devices let you enter information and issue commands.

Examples of input devices include a keyboard, mouse, joystick, modem, microphone and scanner.

PROCESS

The central processing unit (CPU) is the main chip in a computer. It processes instructions, performs calculations and manages the flow of information through a computer system. The CPU communicates with input, output and storage devices to perform tasks.

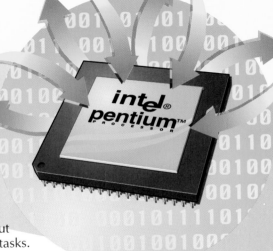

STORE

Like a filing cabinet, a storage device holds information. The computer uses information stored on these devices to perform tasks.

Examples of storage devices include a hard drive, floppy drive, tape drive and CD-ROM drive.

OUTPUT

An output device lets a computer communicate with you. These devices display information on a screen, create printed copies of information or generate sound.

Examples of output devices include a monitor, printer and set of speakers.

THE BASIC COMPUTER

COMPUTER CASE

TYPES OF COMPUTER CASES

The computer case contains all the major components of a computer system.

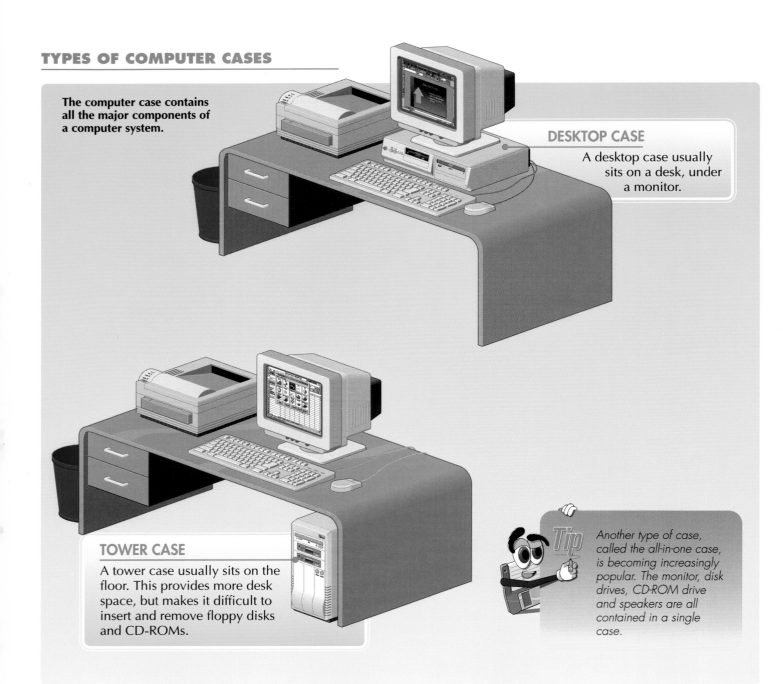

DESKTOP CASE

A desktop case usually sits on a desk, under a monitor.

TOWER CASE

A tower case usually sits on the floor. This provides more desk space, but makes it difficult to insert and remove floppy disks and CD-ROMs.

Tip

Another type of case, called the all-in-one case, is becoming increasingly popular. The monitor, disk drives, CD-ROM drive and speakers are all contained in a single case.

A computer case has buttons that let you easily start or reset the computer.

RESET BUTTON

This button resets a computer without turning the power off and then on again. This button is useful when a computer does not respond to your commands.

POWER BUTTON

This button turns a computer on or off.

HARD DRIVE LIGHT

This light is on when a computer accesses or stores data on the hard drive. Do not move the computer or turn it off when this light is on. This could damage the drive or result in lost data.

COMPUTER CASE

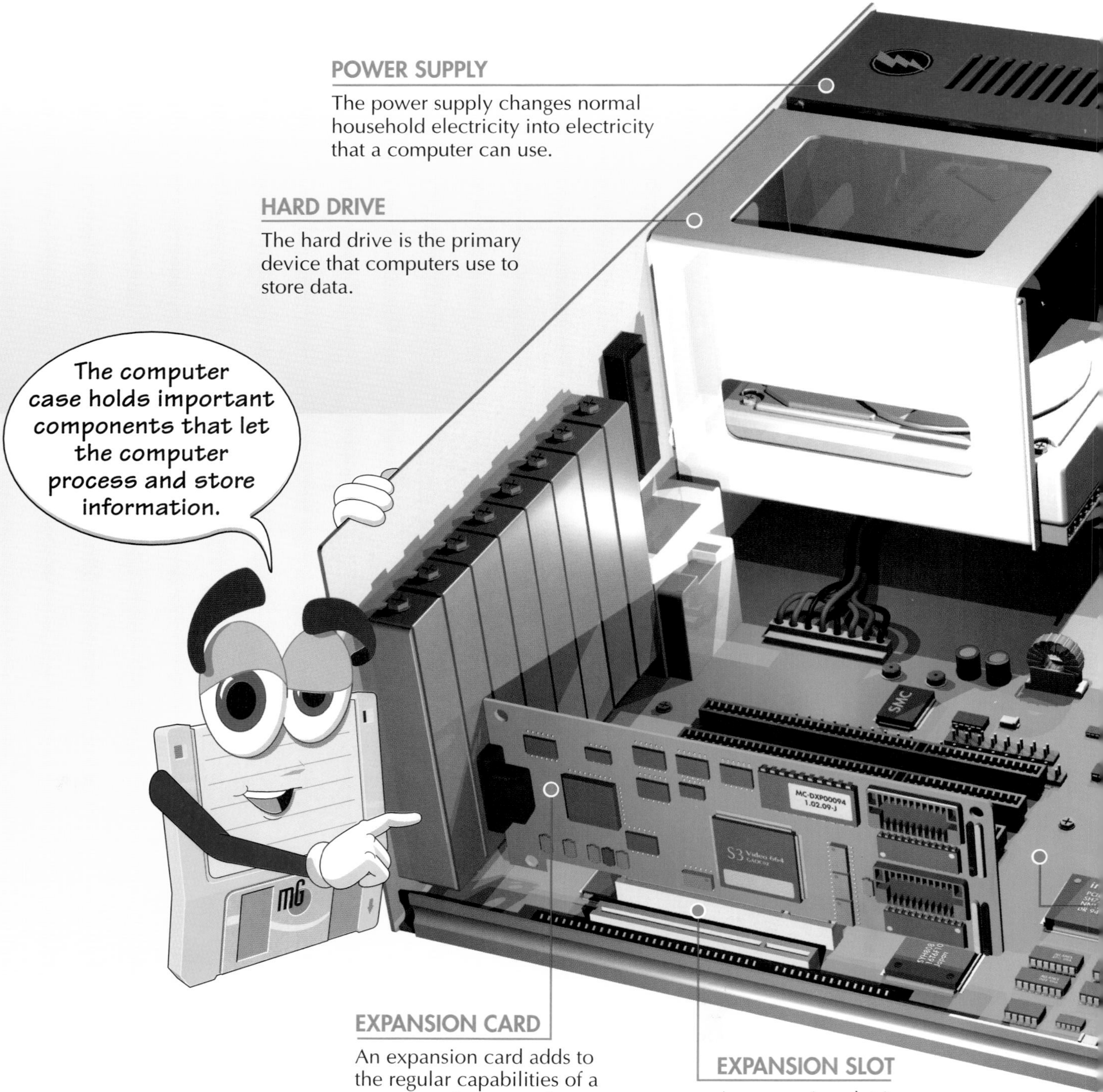

POWER SUPPLY

The power supply changes normal household electricity into electricity that a computer can use.

HARD DRIVE

The hard drive is the primary device that computers use to store data.

The computer case holds important components that let the computer process and store information.

EXPANSION CARD

An expansion card adds to the regular capabilities of a computer. For example, an expansion card can add CD-quality sound.

EXPANSION SLOT

An expansion slot is a socket on the motherboard. An expansion card plugs into an expansion slot.

- • **Computer Case**
- • Ports
- • Power Supply
- • Expansion Cards
- • Bus
- • Plug and Play
- • Ergonomics

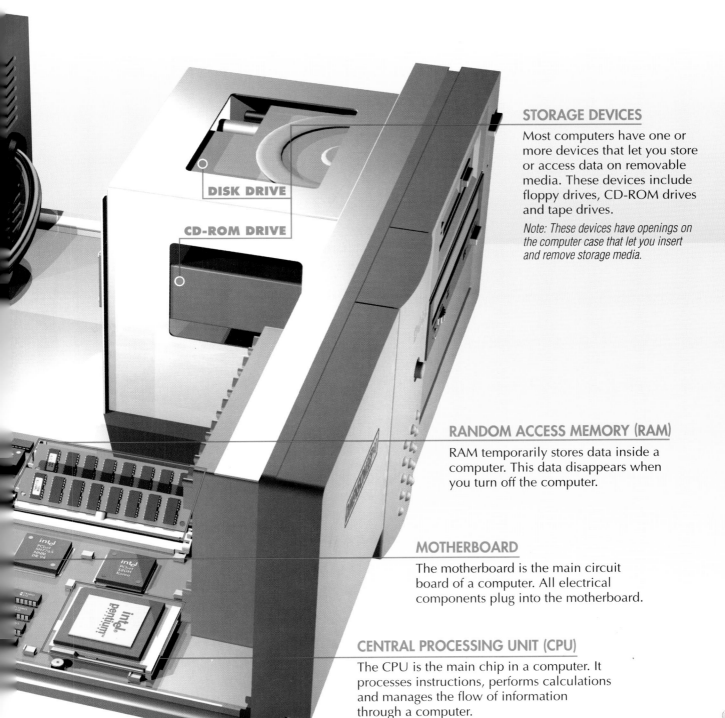

DISK DRIVE

CD-ROM DRIVE

STORAGE DEVICES

Most computers have one or more devices that let you store or access data on removable media. These devices include floppy drives, CD-ROM drives and tape drives.

Note: These devices have openings on the computer case that let you insert and remove storage media.

RANDOM ACCESS MEMORY (RAM)

RAM temporarily stores data inside a computer. This data disappears when you turn off the computer.

MOTHERBOARD

The motherboard is the main circuit board of a computer. All electrical components plug into the motherboard.

CENTRAL PROCESSING UNIT (CPU)

The CPU is the main chip in a computer. It processes instructions, performs calculations and manages the flow of information through a computer.

PORTS

A port is a socket at the back of a computer where you plug in an external device. This lets instructions and data flow between the computer and the device.

SERIAL PORT

A serial port has either 9 or 25 pins and is known as a male connector. This type of port connects a mouse, modem, scanner or occasionally a printer.

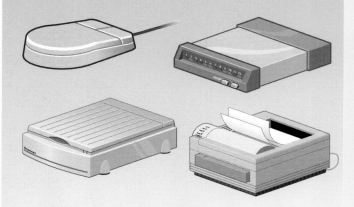

A serial port sends one bit of data, or one-eighth of a character, through a cable at a time. Serial ports can reliably send information more than 20 feet.

A cable that plugs into a serial port has either 9 or 25 holes.

COM

A computer internally labels each serial port with the letters COM. The first serial port is named COM1, the second is named COM2, and so on.

MOUSE PORT

A mouse port connects a mouse.

KEYBOARD PORT

A keyboard port connects a keyboard.

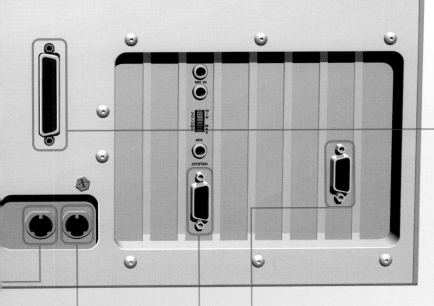

MIC IN

VOLUME MIN MAX

SPK

JOYSTICK

PARALLEL PORT

A parallel port has 25 holes and is known as a female connector. This type of port connects a printer or tape drive.

A parallel port is faster than a serial port. It sends 8 bits of data, or one character, through a cable at a time. Parallel ports cannot reliably send information more than 20 feet.

A cable that plugs into a parallel port has 25 pins.

LPT

A computer internally labels each parallel port with the letters LPT. The first parallel port is named LPT1, the second is named LPT2, and so on.

GAME PORT

A game port connects a joystick.

MONITOR PORT

A monitor port connects a monitor.

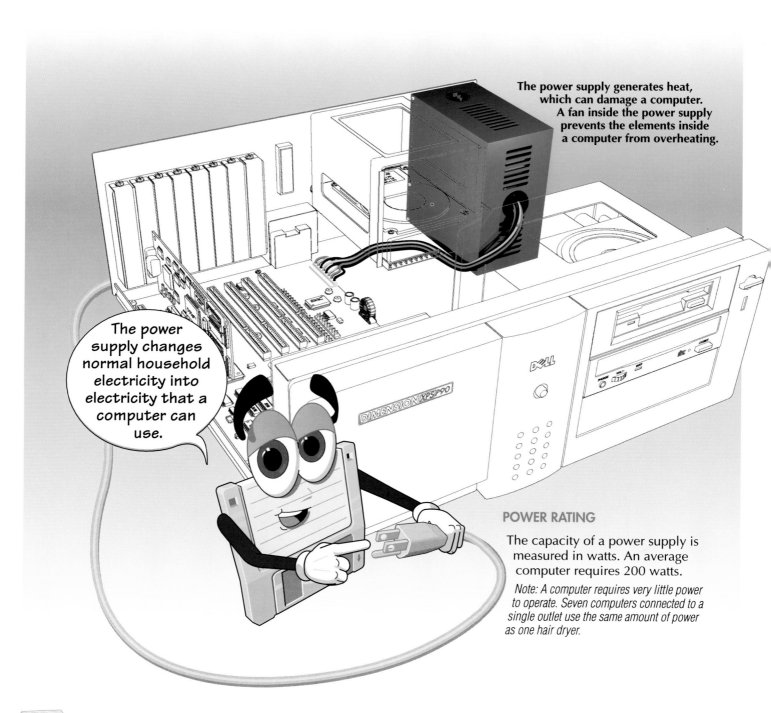

The power supply generates heat, which can damage a computer. A fan inside the power supply prevents the elements inside a computer from overheating.

The power supply changes normal household electricity into electricity that a computer can use.

POWER RATING

The capacity of a power supply is measured in watts. An average computer requires 200 watts.

Note: A computer requires very little power to operate. Seven computers connected to a single outlet use the same amount of power as one hair dryer.

PROTECT YOUR EQUIPMENT

There are two types of power changes that can affect your computer:

• Surges, or fluctuations in power, can occur during storms or when power returns after a power failure

• Power loss

Note: To protect your computer system during electrical storms, detach all cables connecting the computer to a power outlet, network and modem.

POWER BAR

• no protection

A power bar provides additional power outlets. It provides no protection against surges or power loss.

SURGE PROTECTOR

• surge protection

A surge protector guards the computer against surges. Only buy surge protectors that display a "UL1449 approved" label.

UNINTERRUPTIBLE POWER SUPPLY (UPS)

• surge and power loss protection

A UPS protects against surges and power loss. It contains a battery that stores electrical power. If the power fails, the UPS runs the computer for a short time. This gives you time to save your information.

EXPANSION CARDS

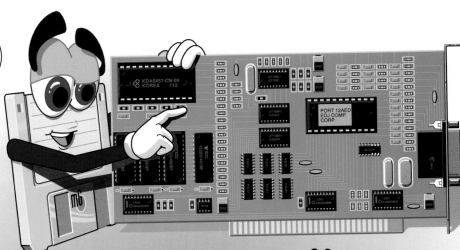

Expansion cards let you add new features to a computer.

Enhanced Graphics

Networking

These are some of the features you can add to a computer.

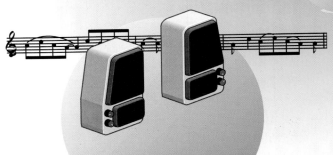

CD-Quality Sound

Modem Communications

- Computer Case
- Ports
- Power Supply
- **Expansion Cards**
- Bus
- Plug and Play
- Ergonomics

ADDING AN EXPANSION CARD

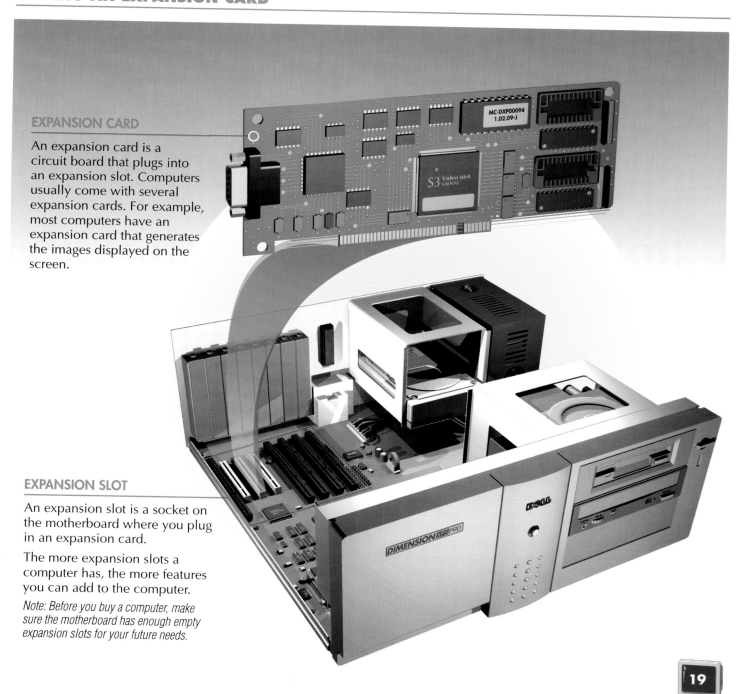

EXPANSION CARD

An expansion card is a circuit board that plugs into an expansion slot. Computers usually come with several expansion cards. For example, most computers have an expansion card that generates the images displayed on the screen.

EXPANSION SLOT

An expansion slot is a socket on the motherboard where you plug in an expansion card.

The more expansion slots a computer has, the more features you can add to the computer.

Note: Before you buy a computer, make sure the motherboard has enough empty expansion slots for your future needs.

BUS

The bus is the electronic pathway in a computer that carries information between devices. There are three types of buses.

◆ Most 486 computers have a VL-Bus and an ISA bus.

Note: 486 refers to the type of central processing unit (CPU) in a computer. The CPU is the main processing chip.

ISA BUS

The Industry Standard Architecture (ISA) bus is the oldest and least expensive type of bus. This bus is ideal for transferring information to and from slow devices, such as a modem.

Bus width - 16 bits
Bus speed - 8 MHz

VL-BUS

The VL-Bus transfers information much faster than the ISA bus. This bus is primarily used to send data to a monitor for fast display of graphical information.

Bus width - 32 bits
Bus speed - 33 MHz

- Computer Case
- Ports
- Power Supply
- Expansion Cards
- Bus
- Plug and Play
- Ergonomics

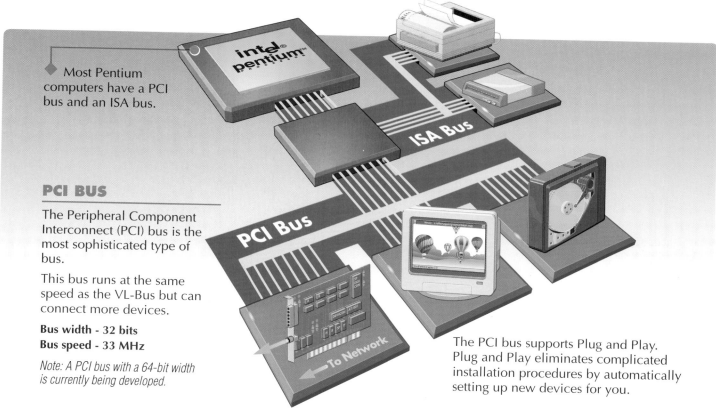

◆ Most Pentium computers have a PCI bus and an ISA bus.

PCI BUS

The Peripheral Component Interconnect (PCI) bus is the most sophisticated type of bus.

This bus runs at the same speed as the VL-Bus but can connect more devices.

Bus width - 32 bits
Bus speed - 33 MHz

Note: A PCI bus with a 64-bit width is currently being developed.

The PCI bus supports Plug and Play. Plug and Play eliminates complicated installation procedures by automatically setting up new devices for you.

Each bus has a specific width and speed.

The **bus width** is similar to the number of lanes on a highway. The greater the width, the more data that can flow along the bus at a time. Width is measured in bits. Eight bits equal one character.

The **bus speed** is similar to the speed limit on a highway. The higher the speed, the faster data travels along the bus. Speed is measured in megahertz (MHz).

PLUG AND PLAY

Plug and Play (PnP) lets you easily add new features to a computer and immediately use them.

BEFORE PLUG AND PLAY

Before Plug and Play, adding new features to a computer was a difficult and frustrating task. Plug and Play eliminates complicated installation procedures by automatically setting up new features for you.

PLUG AND PLAY ELEMENTS

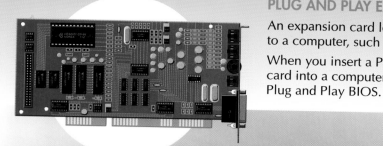

PLUG AND PLAY EXPANSION CARD

An expansion card lets you add a new feature to a computer, such as CD-quality sound.

When you insert a Plug and Play expansion card into a computer, it identifies itself to the Plug and Play BIOS.

PLUG AND PLAY BIOS

The Plug and Play BIOS (Basic Input-Output System) is a chip on the motherboard. It senses when you add or remove an expansion card and immediately notifies the operating system.

PLUG AND PLAY OPERATING SYSTEM

The operating system is a program that controls the overall activity of a computer.

A Plug and Play operating system automatically sets up new devices that the BIOS detects.

Note: Windows 95 supports Plug and Play. Earlier versions of Windows do not support Plug and Play.

ERGONOMICS

Ergonomics is the science
of designing equipment for a
comfortable and safe working
environment.

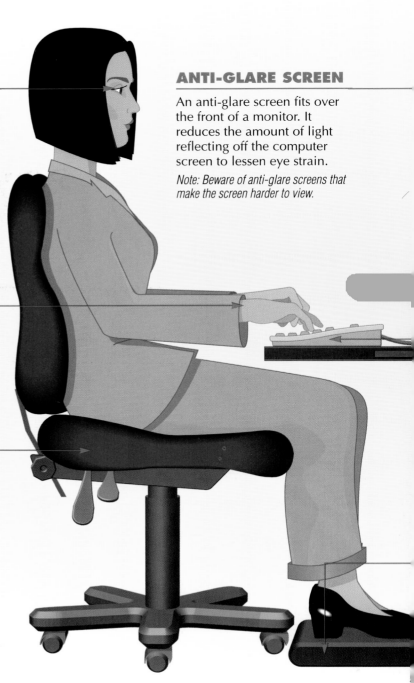

EYES

You should periodically relax your eyes to
prevent eye strain and headaches. To exercise
the muscles in your eyes, focus on a distant
object, then focus on a close object. Repeat
this several times. Perform this exercise a few
times each hour.

WRISTS

Your wrists should be higher than your
fingers and should remain straight at all
times. You can buy a wrist rest to elevate
your wrists and ensure they remain
straight.

CHAIR

Look for a fully adjustable chair that
provides support for your lower back.
Do not lean forward or slouch in the
chair. You should shift positions every
now and then. Once an hour, stand up
and stretch your arms and legs.

ANTI-GLARE SCREEN

An anti-glare screen fits over
the front of a monitor. It
reduces the amount of light
reflecting off the computer
screen to lessen eye strain.

*Note: Beware of anti-glare screens that
make the screen harder to view.*

- Computer Case
- Ports
- Power Supply
- Expansion Cards
- Bus
- Plug and Play
- **Ergonomics**

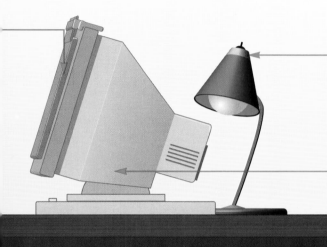

LIGHTING

Overhead lights reflect light off the computer screen, which can cause eye strain. A desk light or track light that is not directly pointed at the screen will help reduce eye strain.

MONITOR

The top edge of the monitor should be at eye level or slightly lower. Most monitors have a tilt-and-swivel base that lets you adjust the angle of the screen.

KEYBOARD

While you type, your elbows should be level with the keyboard. You can buy a keyboard holder that lets you adjust the height of the keyboard. It also provides additional desk space.

FOOT REST

Make sure your feet are flat on the floor. If your feet do not reach the floor, buy a foot rest or try placing your feet on a telephone book.

CARPAL TUNNEL SYNDROME

Carpal Tunnel Syndrome (CTS) is a condition of numbness, tingling and pain in the fingers. This condition affects some workers who type without proper wrist support or type for long periods of time without breaks.

INPUT AND OUTPUT

· ·

Keyboard

Mouse

Monitor and Video Adapter

Printer

Modem

Scanner

Sound Card

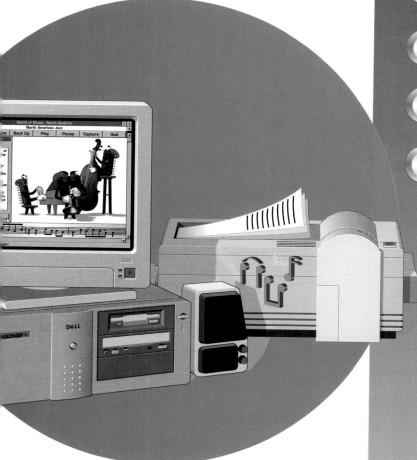

KEYBOARD

You can use the keyboard to enter information and instructions into a computer.

FUNCTION KEYS

These keys let you quickly perform specific tasks. For example, in many programs, you can press **F1** to display help information.

ESCAPE KEY

You can press **Esc** to quit a task you are performing.

CAPS LOCK AND SHIFT KEYS

These keys let you enter text in upper (ABCD) and lower (abcd) case letters.

Press **Caps Lock** to change the case of all letters you type. Press the key again to return to the original case.

Press **Shift** in combination with another key to type an uppercase letter.

CTRL AND ALT KEYS

You can use the **Ctrl** or **Alt** key with another key to perform a specific task. For example, in some programs, you can press **Ctrl+S** to save a document.

SPACEBAR

You can press the **Spacebar** to insert a blank space.

Note:
Your keyboard may look different from the keyboard shown here.

- **Keyboard**
- Mouse
- Monitor and Video Adapter
- Printer
- Modem
- Scanner
- Sound Card

BACKSPACE KEY

You can press **Backspace** to remove the character to the left of the cursor.

STATUS LIGHTS

These lights indicate whether the **Num Lock** or **Caps Lock** features are on or off.

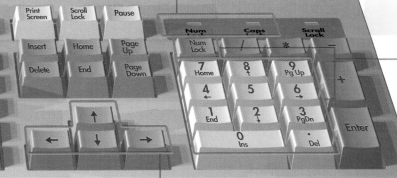

NUMERIC KEYPAD

When the **Num Lock** light is on, you can use the number keys (0 through 9) to enter numbers. When the **Num Lock** light is off, you can use these keys to move the cursor around the screen. To turn the light on or off, press **Num Lock**.

ENTER KEY

You can press **Enter** to tell the computer to carry out a task. In a word processing program, press this key to start a new paragraph.

ARROW KEYS

These keys let you easily move the cursor around the screen.

Tips

- Many programs tell you to "press any key to continue." This simply means press the *Spacebar*.

- Most keyboards have small bumps on the *D* and *K* keys or on the *F* and *J* keys. These bumps help you position your fingers without looking at the keyboard.

- There are programs available to help you improve your typing skills. You can buy these programs at most computer stores.

MOUSE

PARTS OF THE MOUSE

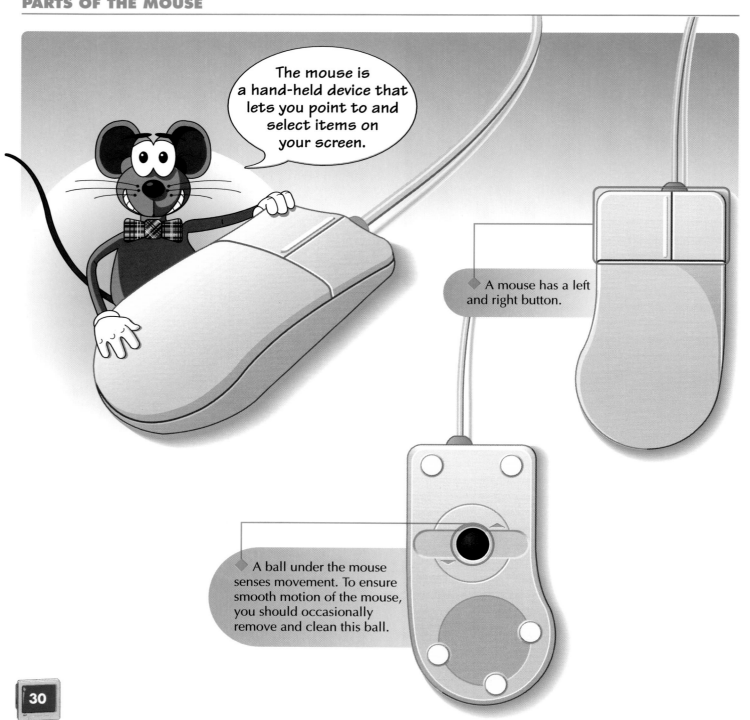

The mouse is a hand-held device that lets you point to and select items on your screen.

A mouse has a left and right button.

A ball under the mouse senses movement. To ensure smooth motion of the mouse, you should occasionally remove and clean this ball.

- Keyboard
- *Mouse*
- Monitor and Video Adapter
- Printer
- Modem
- Scanner
- Sound Card

USING THE MOUSE

Hold the mouse as shown in the diagram. Use your thumb and two rightmost fingers to move the mouse while your two remaining fingers press the mouse buttons.

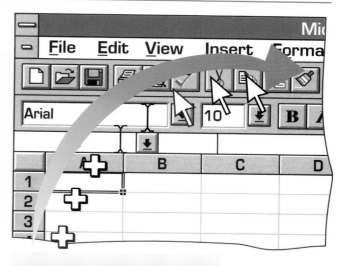

When you move the mouse on your desk, the mouse pointer on the screen moves in the same direction.

MOUSE POINTER

The mouse pointer assumes different shapes, depending on its location on the screen and the task you are performing.

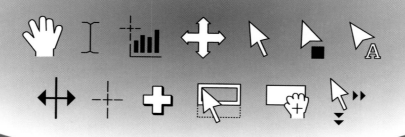

MOUSE

MOUSE TERMS

CLICK

Press and release the left mouse button.

DOUBLE CLICK

Quickly press and release the left mouse button twice.

DRAG AND DROP

When the mouse pointer is over an object on the screen, press and hold down the left mouse button. Still holding down the button, move the mouse to where you want to place the object and then release the button.

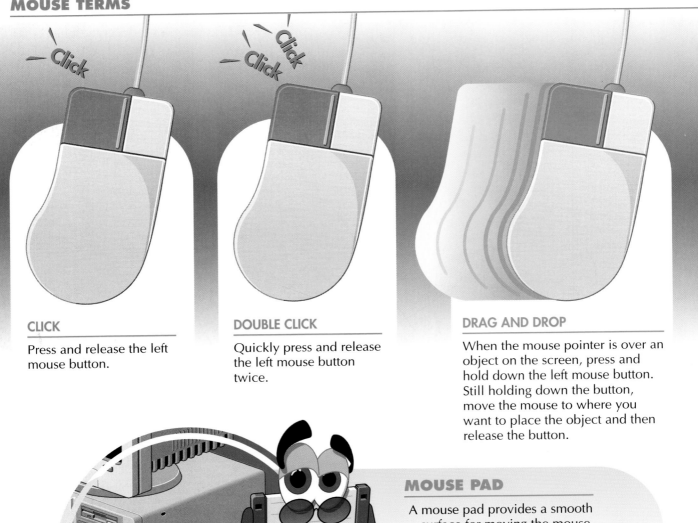

MOUSE PAD

A mouse pad provides a smooth surface for moving the mouse on your desk. You can buy mouse pads displaying interesting designs or pictures at most computer stores.

- Keyboard
- **Mouse**
- Monitor and Video Adapter
- Printer
- Modem
- Scanner
- Sound Card

Tip Most programs sold today are designed to work with a mouse. A mouse is essential when using Windows programs.

CORDLESS MOUSE

A cordless mouse reduces the clutter on your desk by eliminating the mouse cord. This type of mouse runs on a battery. When you move the mouse on your desk, it sends signals through the air to your computer, the same way a television converter sends signals to a television.

TRACKBALL

A trackball is an upside-down mouse that remains stationary on your desk. You roll the ball with your fingers or palm to move the mouse pointer on the screen. A trackball is a great alternative to a mouse when you have limited desk space.

The monitor and video adapter work together to display text and images on the screen.

MONITOR

A monitor displays text and images generated by the video adapter.

KRYO

◆ A cable connects the monitor and video adapter.

VIDEO ADAPTER

The video adapter is an expansion card that plugs into the motherboard. It translates instructions from the CPU into a form the monitor can understand.

CPU

The central processing unit (CPU) sends instructions and data to the video adapter.

- Keyboard
- Mouse
- **Monitor and Video Adapter**
- Printer
- Modem
- Scanner
- Sound Card

CHOOSING A MONITOR

SIZE

The size of a monitor is measured diagonally across the screen. The standard monitor size is 14 or 15 inches. Larger monitors display more information on the screen but are more expensive.

DOT PITCH

The dot pitch measures the clarity of a monitor. The smaller the dot pitch, the crisper the images on the screen. Select a monitor with a dot pitch of 0.28 mm or less.

CONTROLS

Monitors have controls that let you adjust the images on the screen.

For information on more features, refer to the next page.

Monitors offer a wide range of features. You can choose a monitor to suit your needs and budget.

CHOOSING A MONITOR (CONTINUED)

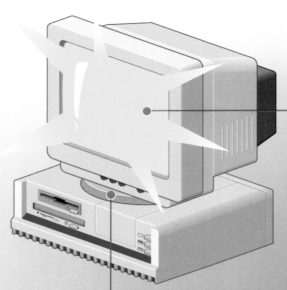

NON-INTERLACED MONITOR

A non-interlaced monitor greatly reduces screen flicker. These monitors are more expensive than interlaced monitors but reduce eye strain.

ANTI-GLARE SCREEN

An anti-glare screen fits over the front of a monitor. It helps reduce the amount of light reflected off the computer screen. Some monitors come with etched or coated glass that acts as a built-in anti-glare screen.

TILT-AND-SWIVEL BASE

A tilt-and-swivel base lets you adjust the angle of the screen. This lets you reduce the glare from overhead lighting and view the screen more comfortably.

ENERGY STAR

To reduce energy use, the Environmental Protection Agency (EPA) developed an energy-saving guideline called Energy Star. When an Energy Star computer is idle for a period of time, it enters an energy-saving sleep mode.

To find an Energy Star computer, monitor or printer, look for the ENERGY STAR™ logo.

- Keyboard
- Mouse
- **Monitor and Video Adapter**
- Printer
- Modem
- Scanner
- Sound Card

ELECTROMAGNETIC RADIATION

Monitors emit electromagnetic radiation (EMR). You can protect yourself from the potentially harmful effects by turning off your monitor when you are not using it and buying monitors that meet MPR II guidelines. These guidelines define acceptable levels of EMR.

The screen technology used in portable computers does not emit electromagnetic radiation.

Note: Many home appliances also emit electromagnetic radiation, including microwaves, TVs and radios.

SCREEN SAVERS

A screen saver is a moving picture or pattern that appears on the screen when you do not use your computer for a period of time.

Screen savers were originally designed to prevent screen burn, which occurs when an image appears in a fixed position for a period of time.

Today's monitors are better designed to prevent screen burn, although people still use screen savers for their entertainment value.

Note: Windows provides several screen savers. You can purchase more sophisticated screen savers at most computer stores.

MONITOR AND VIDEO ADAPTER

Resolution determines the amount of information a monitor can display. It is measured by the number of dots, called pixels, that a monitor can display horizontally and vertically.

Some monitors can display images at only one resolution. **Multisync** monitors can display images at various resolutions. Multisync monitors let you shrink or expand images on a screen to suit your needs.

RESOLUTION

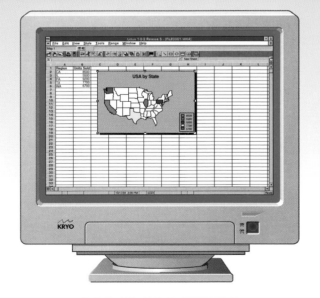

640 X 480 PIXELS

800 X 600 PIXELS

When you use a lower resolution, the images on your screen are larger. This is useful if you have trouble seeing small images.

- Keyboard
- Mouse
- **Monitor and Video Adapter**
- Printer
- Modem
- Scanner
- Sound Card

1,024 X 768 PIXELS

1,280 X 1,024 PIXELS

When you use a higher resolution, the images on your screen are smaller. This is useful if you want to display more information on your screen.

MONITOR AND VIDEO ADAPTER

The number of colors a monitor can display determines how realistic images appear on a screen. More colors result in more realistic images.

COLOR DEPTH

16 COLORS (4-BIT COLOR)

This setting results in choppy-looking color and is considered obsolete.

256 COLORS (8-BIT COLOR)

This setting is ideal for most home and business applications.

- Keyboard
- Mouse
- **Monitor and Video Adapter**
- Printer
- Modem
- Scanner
- Sound Card

VGA (Video Graphics Array) monitors display 16 colors at a resolution of 640 x 480. This is the minimum standard for computer systems.

SVGA (Super Video Graphics Array) monitors display more colors and higher resolutions. Most new computer systems offer SVGA.

65,536 COLORS (16-BIT COLOR)

This setting is ideal for desktop publishing and multimedia applications.

16,777,216 COLORS (24-BIT COLOR)

This setting is also called true color because it displays more colors than the human eye can distinguish. Unless you are a trained professional, it is difficult to distinguish between 16-bit and 24-bit color.

This setting is ideal for photo-retouching and high-end desktop publishing applications.

41

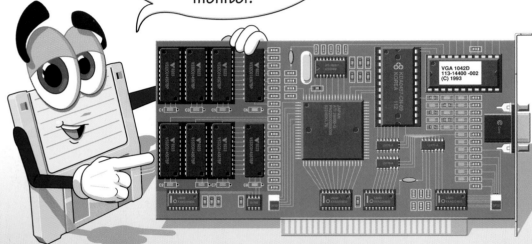

A video adapter has memory chips. These chips temporarily store information before sending it to the monitor.

VIDEO ADAPTER MEMORY

Video adapters use either DRAM or VRAM memory chips.

DRAM
Dynamic Random Access Memory (DRAM) is ideal for routine office tasks.

VRAM
Video Random Access Memory (VRAM) is faster and more expensive than DRAM. VRAM is ideal for high-end applications such as desktop publishing and photo-retouching.

Resolution	Number Of Colors			
	16	256	65,536	16,777,216
640 x 480	256K	512K	1MB	1MB
800 x 600	256K	512K	1MB	2MB
1,024 x 768	512K	1MB	2MB	4MB
1,280 x 1,024	1MB	2MB	4MB	4MB

Note: 1,024K equals 1MB.

The resolution and number of colors a monitor displays determine how much memory the video adapter needs.

Note: For information on resolution and color depth, refer to pages 38 to 41.

- Keyboard
- Mouse
- Monitor and Video Adapter
- Printer
- Modem
- Scanner
- Sound Card

MONITOR AND VIDEO ADAPTER RECOMMENDATIONS

The monitor and video adapter work together to display text and images on the screen.

For best performance, you should choose a monitor and video adapter that best suit your needs.

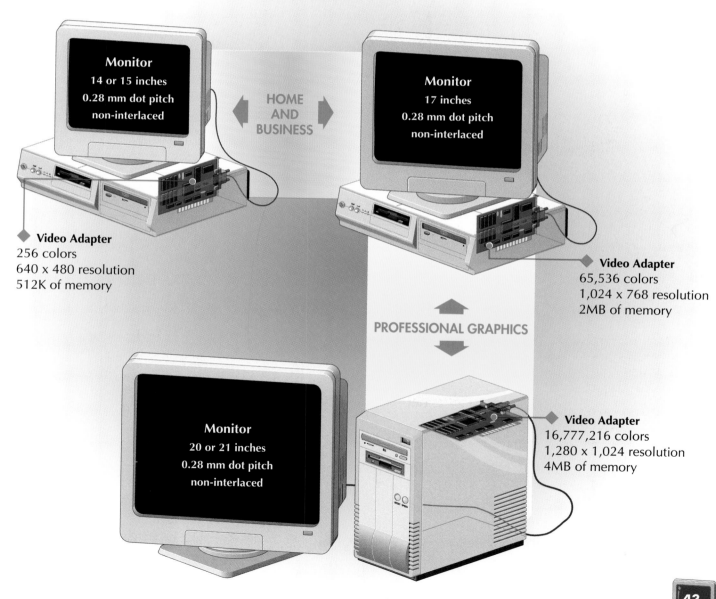

Monitor
14 or 15 inches
0.28 mm dot pitch
non-interlaced

HOME AND BUSINESS

Monitor
17 inches
0.28 mm dot pitch
non-interlaced

◆ **Video Adapter**
256 colors
640 x 480 resolution
512K of memory

◆ **Video Adapter**
65,536 colors
1,024 x 768 resolution
2MB of memory

PROFESSIONAL GRAPHICS

Monitor
20 or 21 inches
0.28 mm dot pitch
non-interlaced

◆ **Video Adapter**
16,777,216 colors
1,280 x 1,024 resolution
4MB of memory

A printer produces a paper copy of the information displayed on a screen.

You can use a printer to produce letters, invoices, newsletters, overhead transparencies, labels, packing slips and much more.

Color printers let you produce documents displaying color, such as overhead transparencies and brochures.

- Keyboard
- Mouse
- Monitor and Video Adapter
- **Printer**
- Modem
- Scanner
- Sound Card

PRINT SPEED AND RESOLUTION

SPEED

The speed of a printer determines how fast it can print the pages you selected. Speed is measured in characters per second (cps) or pages per minute (ppm). A higher speed results in faster output.

Note: A page that contains graphics takes longer to print than a page that contains just text.

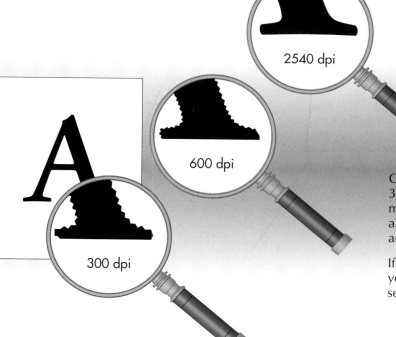

RESOLUTION

The resolution of a printer determines the quality of the images on a printed page. Resolution is measured in dots per inch (dpi). A higher resolution results in sharper, more detailed images.

2540 dpi

600 dpi

300 dpi

Generally, a resolution of 300 dpi is acceptable for most office documents, although 600 dpi printers are becoming more popular.

If you require over 1200 dpi, you can take your work to a service bureau.

PRINTER

CHOOSING A PRINTER

- Keyboard
- Mouse
- Monitor and Video Adapter
- Printer
- Modem
- Scanner
- Sound Card

DOT-MATRIX PRINTER

A dot-matrix printer is the least expensive type of printer. It uses a pattern of tiny dots to form images on a page.

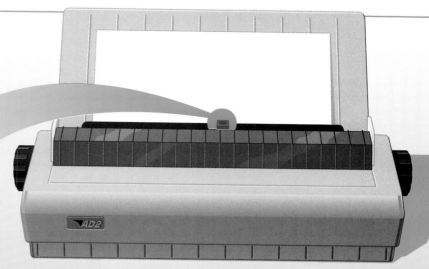

A print head contains small, blunt pins that strike an inked ribbon. This striking action makes a dot-matrix printer quite loud.

You can buy 9-pin or 24-pin dot-matrix printers. The 9-pin printer produces draft quality documents, while the 24-pin printer produces typewriter-like documents.

A dot-matrix printer is ideal for printing on multipart forms, which need an impact to print through multiple copies.

A dot-matrix printer typically uses continuous form paper. This paper has holes punched along each side and connects from end to end.

The print speed of a dot-matrix printer ranges from 200 to 300 characters per second (cps) or 1 to 3 pages per minute (ppm).

SPEED

INK JET PRINTER

An ink jet printer produces high-quality documents at a relatively low price.

Most ink jet printers produce images at 300 dpi at a speed of about one to three pages per minute (ppm).

SPEED

A print head sprays ink on the page through small holes.

Images produced by an ink jet printer take time to dry and may smudge or smear if handled too soon. When purchasing ink for this type of printer, look for smudge-resistant, oil-based ink.

ABC Corporation

100 Sesame Drive, Los Angeles, CA 90032

May 1, 1995

Mr. Tim Grenon
33 Glendon Court
New York, NY 10016

Dear Tim:

Your layout in rough for the new animated commercial was excellent. We're hoping to do almost exactly what you illustrated without changes.

Thanks for doing it so promptly, and we'll surely send more work your way in the future.

Sincerely,
Dave MacDonald

Dave MacDonald
Commercial & Publicity Director

An ink jet printer is ideal for routine business and personal documents.

- Keyboard
- Mouse
- Monitor and Video Adapter
- **Printer**
- Modem
- Scanner
- Sound Card

COLOR INK JET PRINTER

A color ink jet printer is the least expensive type of color printer. It is best suited to add touches of color to documents.

Color ink jet printers can print on plain paper, but produce the best results on special paper with a higher clay content.

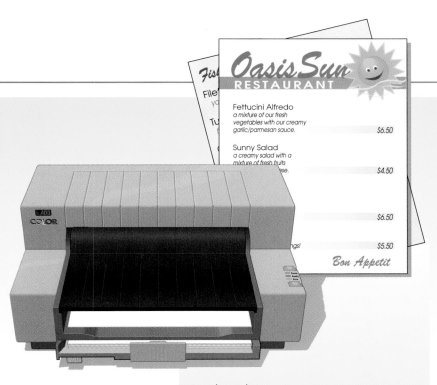

A color ink jet printer sprays cyan, magenta, yellow and black ink to create images on a page. Lower-cost color ink jet printers create black by mixing all the other colors. Look for a printer that offers black as a separate color.

You can print images in one of two directions on a page.

PORTRAIT

Prints images across the short side of the page.

LANDSCAPE

Prints images across the long side of the page.

LASER PRINTER

A laser printer is a high-speed printer that uses a laser beam to form images on a page.

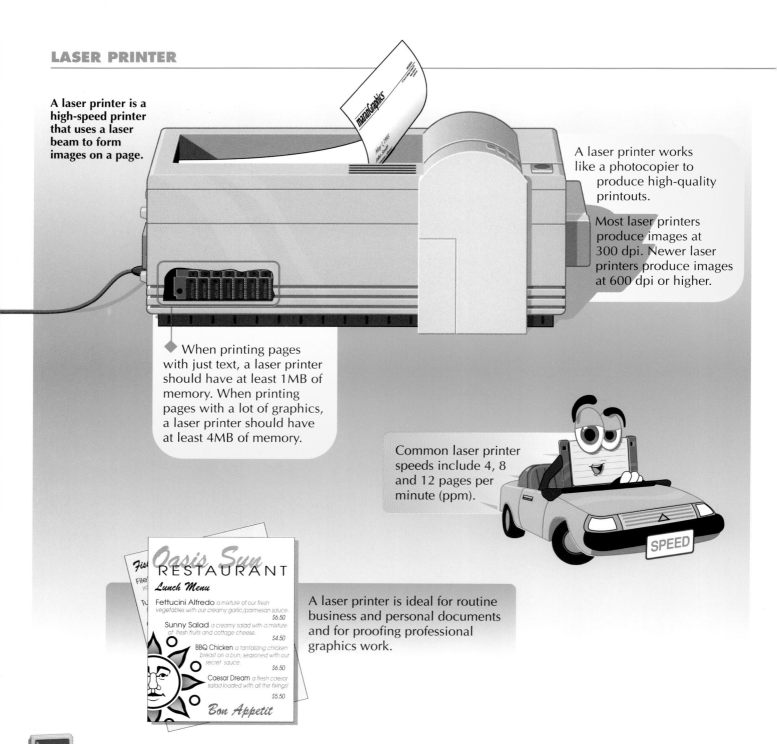

A laser printer works like a photocopier to produce high-quality printouts.

Most laser printers produce images at 300 dpi. Newer laser printers produce images at 600 dpi or higher.

◆ When printing pages with just text, a laser printer should have at least 1MB of memory. When printing pages with a lot of graphics, a laser printer should have at least 4MB of memory.

Common laser printer speeds include 4, 8 and 12 pages per minute (ppm).

A laser printer is ideal for routine business and personal documents and for proofing professional graphics work.

Oasis Sun
RESTAURANT
Lunch Menu

Fettucini Alfredo *a mixture of our fresh vegetables with our creamy garlic/parmesan sauce.*
$6.50

Sunny Salad *a creamy salad with a mixture of fresh fruits and cottage cheese.*
$4.50

BBQ Chicken *a tantalizing chicken breast on a bun, seasoned with our secret sauce.*
$6.50

Caesar Dream *a fresh caesar salad loaded with all the fixings!*
$5.50

Bon Appetit

SPEED

- Keyboard
- Mouse
- Monitor and Video Adapter
- **Printer**
- Modem
- Scanner
- Sound Card

LASER PRINTER LANGUAGES

PCL

A printer control language (PCL) laser printer is less expensive and faster than a PostScript printer. This type of printer is used for routine office tasks.

POSTSCRIPT

A PostScript laser printer provides more capabilities than a PCL printer when you are using various colors, graphics and fonts. This type of printer is popular in the graphic arts industry, especially when the artwork will be sent to a professional print shop.

COLOR LASER PRINTER

A color laser printer is more expensive than a color ink jet printer, but it produces superior output.

PRINTER

THERMAL-WAX COLOR PRINTER

A thermal-wax color printer produces sharp, rich, non-smearing images.

This printer uses three or four full-page ribbons covered with colored wax. A heated print head melts the wax and places it on specially coated, heat-sensitive paper.

Most thermal-wax color printers offer 300 dpi. Some offer up to 600 dpi.

A thermal-wax color printer is ideal for prepress work and for producing color overhead transparencies.

DYE SUBLIMATION COLOR PRINTER

A dye sublimation color printer produces images that look like color photographs.

This printer uses heat to transform the ink from colored ribbons into a gas, which hardens on the page.

Note: Dye sublimation color printers are also called thermal dye transfer printers.

A dye sublimation color printer is ideal for producing high-quality color documents.

PRINT SPOOLER AND PRINT BUFFER

A computer can send data faster than a printer can accept and process the data. A print spooler or print buffer acts like a dam, holding the data and then releasing it at a speed the printer can handle.

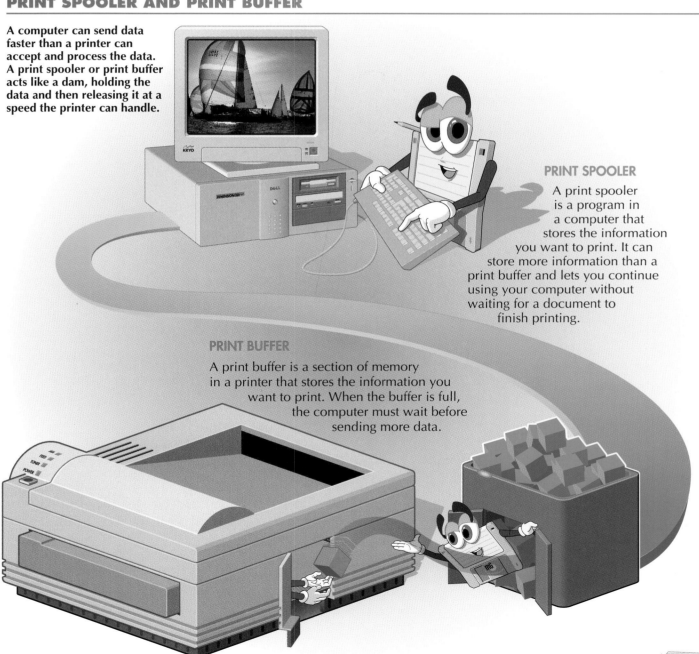

PRINT SPOOLER

A print spooler is a program in a computer that stores the information you want to print. It can store more information than a print buffer and lets you continue using your computer without waiting for a document to finish printing.

PRINT BUFFER

A print buffer is a section of memory in a printer that stores the information you want to print. When the buffer is full, the computer must wait before sending more data.

MODEM

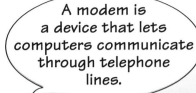

A modem is a device that lets computers communicate through telephone lines.

MODEM

FAX SERVICES

You can buy a modem with fax capabilities. A fax modem lets you send information from a computer to a fax machine or to another fax modem.

When a computer receives a fax, the document appears on the screen. You can review and print the document, but you cannot edit it unless you have special optical character recognition (OCR) software.

Using a fax modem to send a document is faster than printing it and then using a fax machine to send the document.

- Keyboard
- Mouse
- Monitor and Video Adapter
- Printer
- Modem
- Scanner
- Sound Card

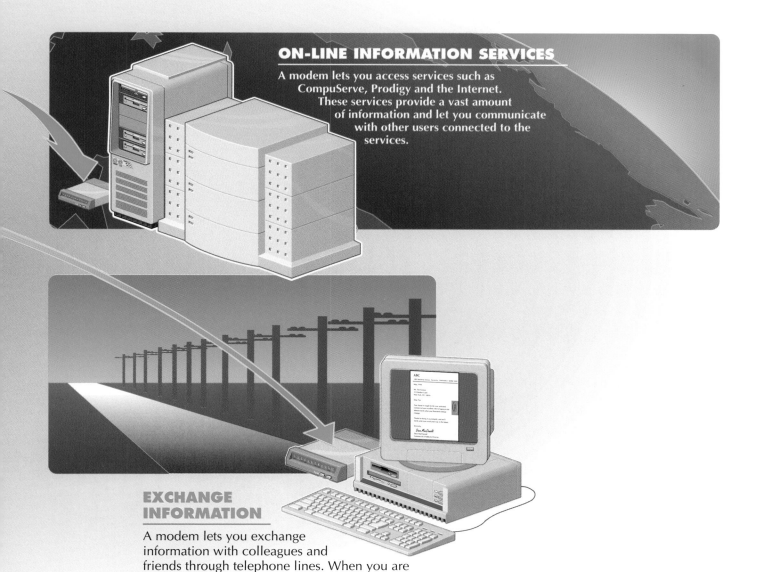

ON-LINE INFORMATION SERVICES

A modem lets you access services such as CompuServe, Prodigy and the Internet. These services provide a vast amount of information and let you communicate with other users connected to the services.

EXCHANGE INFORMATION

A modem lets you exchange information with colleagues and friends through telephone lines. When you are at home or traveling, you can use a modem to access information stored on your computer at work.

MODEM

INTERNAL MODEM

You can see the edge of an internal modem at the back of a computer. A telephone line plugs into a jack on the modem.

An internal modem is inside a computer. It is usually less expensive than an external modem.

◆ An internal modem plugs into an expansion slot inside a computer.

HANDSHAKE

Two modems perform a handshake just as two people shake hands to greet each other. A handshake establishes how the modems will exchange data.

COMMUNICATIONS PROGRAM

A communications program manages the transmission of data between two modems. This software usually comes with a modem.

EXTERNAL MODEM

> An external modem sits outside the computer in its own case. An external modem is portable, so you can easily use it with different computers.

HS AA CD OH RD SD TR MR

POWER

◆ Status lights on the modem tell you about the current transmission. For example, RD stands for receiving data.

RS-232   Line Phone

◆ A cable plugs into this port to connect the modem and the computer.

◆ A telephone line plugs into the modem.

◆ The modem plugs into a power outlet.

Tip

When buying an external modem, make sure your computer's serial port (the socket at the back of a computer where you connect a modem) has a 16550 UART. The 16550 UART controls the flow of information to and from the modem and allows for fast transmission of data.

MODEM

SPEED

> The speed that a modem can transmit data through telephone lines is the most important consideration when buying a modem.

Modem standards ensure that modems made by different manufacturers can communicate with each other.

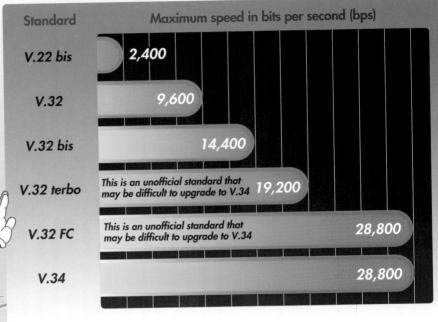

Standard	Maximum speed in bits per second (bps)
V.22 bis	2,400
V.32	9,600
V.32 bis	14,400
V.32 terbo	This is an unofficial standard that may be difficult to upgrade to V.34 — 19,200
V.32 FC	This is an unofficial standard that may be difficult to upgrade to V.34 — 28,800
V.34	28,800

Note: The word "bis" means "version 2" or "second."

Faster modems cost more but will save you time and money in the long run. When transferring files, faster modems take less time to transfer the data. This saves you money on long distance charges and on-line service charges.

Modems must use the same speed when exchanging data. A fast modem can talk to a slower modem, but they will communicate at the slower speed.

- Keyboard
- Mouse
- Monitor and Video Adapter
- Printer
- **Modem**
- Scanner
- Sound Card

COMPRESSION

A modem can compress or squeeze data being sent to another modem. This speeds up the transfer of data.

Standard	Speed Enhancement
MNP 5	2X FASTER
MNP 7	3X FASTER
V.42 bis	4X FASTER

To use compression, both the sending and receiving modems must use the same compression standard.

ERROR CONTROL

Modems can provide error control to ensure that data sent between modems is accurate. If a modem detects an error in the data being sent by another modem, it will ask the modem to resend the data.

Standard	Use
MNP 2, 3, 4	*These standards are used with older modems.*
V.42	*This standard is used with newer modems. It includes MNP 2, 3 and 4.*

SCANNER

A scanner translates the information it sees on a page into a format the computer can use.

A scanner is like a photocopier, except it creates a computer file instead of a paper copy.

After you scan an image into a computer, you can edit or print the image.

SCANNER APPLICATIONS

TEXT

Scanners with special optical character recognition (OCR) software can read handwritten or printed text. OCR software interprets the lines and squiggles on a page and converts them into characters. This provides a quick way to enter printed text into your computer.

ABC Corporation Newsletter

ILLUSTRATIONS

You can use a scanner to import diagrams and sketches into a document. For example, you can scan a map into your computer and then use the map in a newsletter.

- Keyboard
- Mouse
- Monitor and Video Adapter
- Printer
- Modem
- Scanner
- Sound Card

TYPES OF SCANNERS

HAND-HELD SCANNER

A hand-held scanner is less expensive than a flatbed scanner. It is ideal for importing small images, such as signatures and logos.

To scan an image, you slide the scanner over the image. You must move your hand smoothly to produce a clear picture on the computer screen.

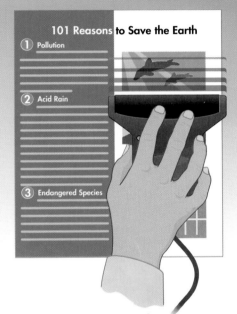

FLATBED SCANNER

A flatbed scanner works like a photocopier. It can import an entire page at once and produce clearer images on a computer screen than a hand-held scanner.

To scan an image, you place the image face down on the scanner.

61

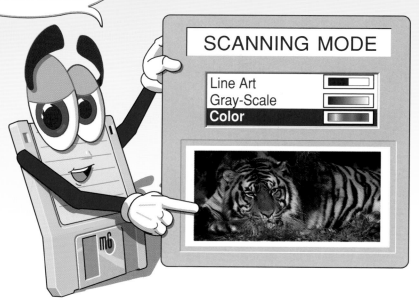

When scanning an image, you need to select a scanning mode and resolution.

SCANNING MODE

Line Art
Gray-Scale
Color

SCANNING MODE

A scanner offers three scanning modes.

RESOLUTION

A scanner lets you specify the resolution you want to use. The resolution refers to the amount of detail a scanner can detect. A higher resolution results in more detailed scanned images but requires more scanning time and storage space. Resolution is measured in dots per inch (dpi).

Note: There is no need to scan an image beyond the resolution of the printer you will be using. For example, if you plan on printing a scanned image on a 300 dpi printer, do not scan the image at a resolution higher than 300 dpi.

- Keyboard
- Mouse
- Monitor and Video Adapter
- Printer
- Modem
- **Scanner**
- Sound Card

LINE ART
This mode scans an image using just black and white.

GRAY-SCALE
This mode scans an image using black, white and shades of gray.

COLOR
This mode scans an image using shades of red, blue and green.

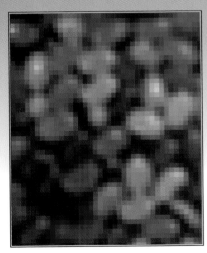

20 dpi

60 dpi

300 dpi

SOUND CARD

A sound card improves the sound quality of a computer.

A sound card plugs into an expansion slot inside a computer.

Without a sound card, a computer can only produce beeps and muffled sounds through an internal speaker.

Tip
A sound card is also called a sound board or audio card.

- Keyboard
- Mouse
- Monitor and Video Adapter
- Printer
- Modem
- Scanner
- **Sound Card**

CHOOSING A SOUND CARD

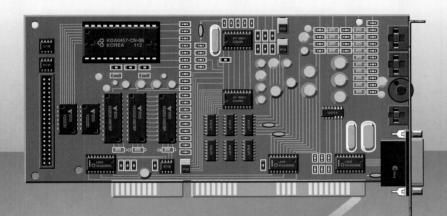

For CD-quality sound, purchase a 16-bit, 44.1kHz sound card that is Sound Blaster-compatible. If possible, listen to the sounds produced by various sound cards before making your purchase.

Note: 8-bit sound cards produce lower quality sound and are now considered obsolete.

SOUND CARD APPLICATIONS

GAMES

When playing games, a sound card lets you hear music, speech and sound effects.

To use a sound card with most DOS-based games, make sure it is Sound Blaster-compatible.

To use a sound card with Windows-based games, make sure it comes with software that works with Windows.

RECORD SOUNDS

A sound card lets you add music and speech to documents and presentations. It also lets you use a computer to compose music.

SOUND CARD

SOUND CARD CONNECTIONS

You can see the edge of a sound card at the back of a computer. A sound card has several ports where you can plug in external devices.

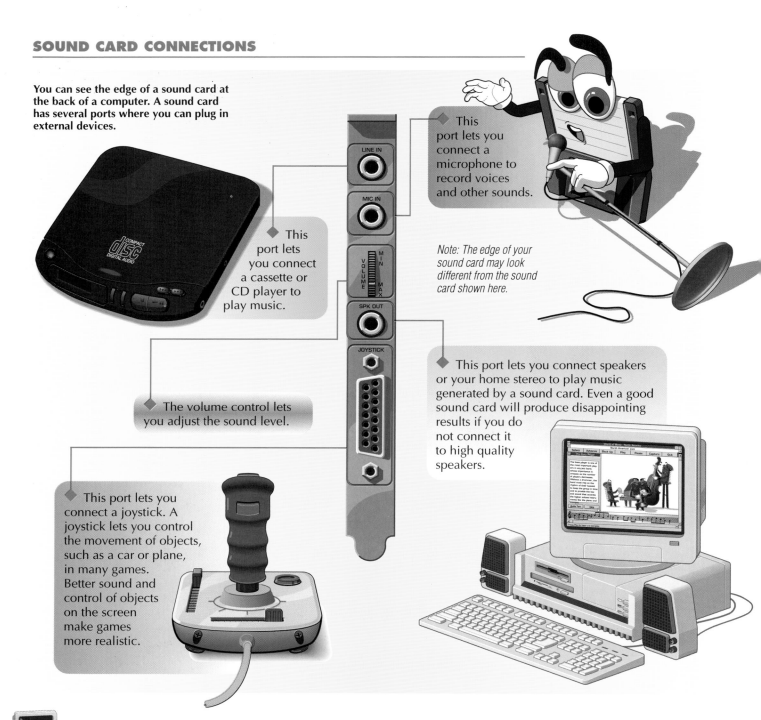

This port lets you connect a microphone to record voices and other sounds.

This port lets you connect a cassette or CD player to play music.

Note: The edge of your sound card may look different from the sound card shown here.

The volume control lets you adjust the sound level.

This port lets you connect speakers or your home stereo to play music generated by a sound card. Even a good sound card will produce disappointing results if you do not connect it to high quality speakers.

This port lets you connect a joystick. A joystick lets you control the movement of objects, such as a car or plane, in many games. Better sound and control of objects on the screen make games more realistic.

LINE IN

MIC IN

VOLUME MIN MAX

SPK OUT

JOYSTICK

- Keyboard
- Mouse
- Monitor and Video Adapter
- Printer
- Modem
- Scanner
- **Sound Card**

MIDI

Musical Instrument Digital Interface (MIDI) is a set of rules that allow computers, synthesizers and musical instruments to exchange data. This lets you use a computer to play, record and edit music.

Note: A synthesizer is a keyboard instrument that electronically produces speech, music and other sounds.

Many musicians use MIDI to compose music on a computer.

A sound card that supports MIDI ensures that a computer can generate the sounds often found in games, CD-ROM titles and presentation packages.

FM AND WAVETABLE SYNTHESIS

There are two ways a sound card can produce MIDI sound.

FM synthesis produces unrealistic, tinny sound by imitating the sounds of musical instruments.

Wavetable synthesis produces rich, realistic sound by using actual recordings of musical instruments.

Wavetable synthesis is more costly than FM synthesis but produces superior sound.

PROCESSING

- Memory
- Central Processing Unit
- Memory Cache

,654

CPU

MEMORY

Memory, also called Random Access Memory (RAM), temporarily stores data inside a computer.

Memory works like a blackboard that is constantly overwritten with new data.

The amount of memory, or memory size, in a computer determines the number of programs you can run at once. Memory size also determines how fast your programs will operate.

The data stored in memory is temporary and disappears when you turn off the computer.

MEASURING MEMORY

Bytes are used to measure memory and the capacity of storage devices such as floppy disks and hard drives.

BYTE

One character. A character can be a number, letter or symbol.

Note: A byte consists of 8 bits.

KILOBYTE (K)

Approximately one thousand characters, or one page of double spaced text.

MEGABYTE (MB)

Approximately one million characters, or one novel.

GIGABYTE (GB)

Approximately one billion characters, or one thousand novels.

Tip

If you are using Windows programs for routine office tasks, your computer must have at least 8MB of memory for adequate performance.

MEMORY

TYPES OF MEMORY

A computer can have up to three types of memory.

VRAM

Video RAM (VRAM) is slightly faster and more expensive than DRAM.

Video adapters with VRAM are used for high-end applications such as desktop publishing and photo-retouching. Lower-cost video adapters with DRAM are used for routine office tasks.

Note: A video adapter uses VRAM or DRAM to store an image before sending it to the monitor.

SRAM

Static RAM (SRAM) works at very high speeds and is the most expensive type of memory.

SRAM improves the performance of the central processing unit (CPU) by storing data recently used by the CPU. This lets the CPU quickly retrieve the data it needs.

DRAM

Dynamic RAM (DRAM) is relatively inexpensive and is used for the computer's main memory. You can improve the performance of a computer by adding more DRAM.

ADDING MEMORY

SIMM

A SIMM is a circuit board that holds DRAM chips.

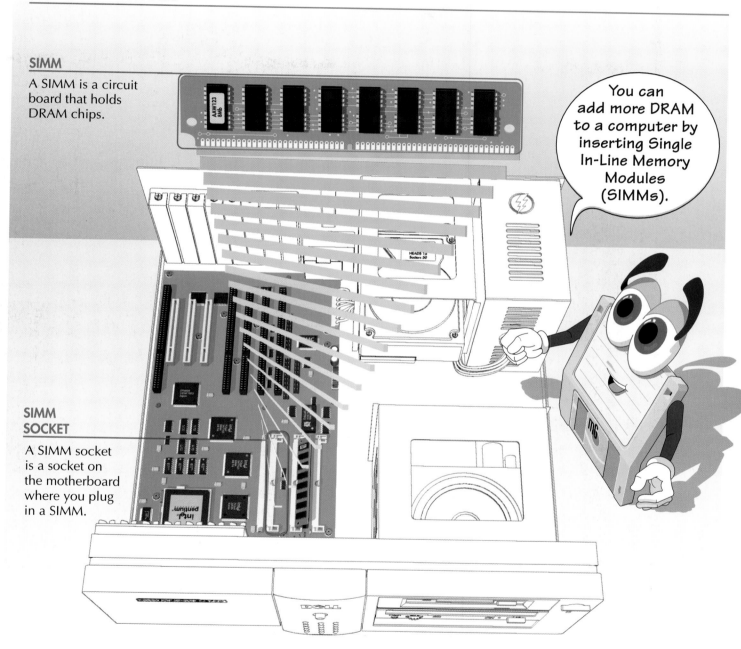

You can add more DRAM to a computer by inserting Single In-Line Memory Modules (SIMMs).

SIMM SOCKET

A SIMM socket is a socket on the motherboard where you plug in a SIMM.

CPU

The CPU performs millions of calculations every second. With the guidance of software programs and your instructions, the CPU lets you perform a wide variety of tasks, from writing a letter to balancing a checkbook.

Note: The CPU is also called a microprocessor.

- Memory
- **Central Processing Unit**
- Memory Cache

MANUFACTURER

CPUs are made by companies such as Intel, IBM, AMD and Cyrix. Intel CPUs are the most popular.

GENERATION

Each new generation of CPUs is more powerful than the one before. CPU generations include the 386, 486 and Pentium.

TYPE

The 486 generation of CPUs is available in four different types. These types include the 486SX, 486DX, 486DX2 and the 486DX4.

SPEED

Each CPU generation is available in several speeds. For example, the 486 generation is available in speeds ranging from 33MHz to 100MHz.

Note: CPU generation, type and speed are further explained on the following pages.

Tip

CPUs operate at either 3.3V or 5V (Volts). The newer 3.3V chips use less than half as much power as the 5V chips.

Portable computers and energy saving desktop computers use the 3.3V chip.

CENTRAL PROCESSING UNIT

Each new generation of CPUs is faster and more powerful than the previous generation.

CPU GENERATION

386
This chip is found in old computers. It is now obsolete.

486
This chip provides good performance for most tasks.

PENTIUM
This chip is more expensive than a 486 but provides superior performance.

P6
This chip is more expensive than a Pentium but offers even better performance.

Each new generation of CPUs can process more instructions at a time than the previous generation.

This chip processes one instruction at a time.

This chip processes two instructions at a time. It is twice as fast as a 486.

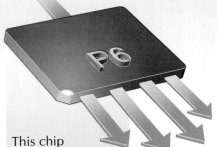

This chip processes four instructions at a time. It is twice as fast as a Pentium.

The CPU speed is a major factor in determining how fast a computer operates.

CPU SPEED

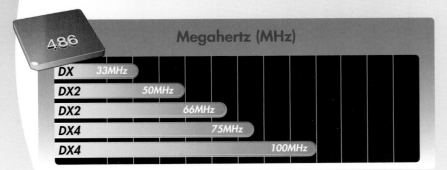

486 — Megahertz (MHz)

DX — 33MHz
DX2 — 50MHz
DX2 — 66MHz
DX4 — 75MHz
DX4 — 100MHz

The speed of a CPU is measured in megahertz (MHz), which indicates millions of cycles per second.

Each CPU generation is available in several speeds. The faster the speed, the faster the computer operates.

Note: Some 486 and Pentium CPUs operate at the same speed. However, Pentium CPUs always provide superior performance because they process more instructions at a time.

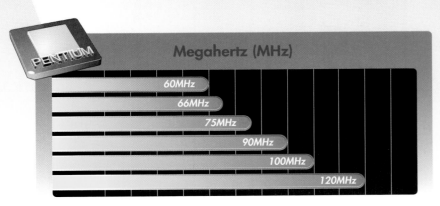

PENTIUM — Megahertz (MHz)

60MHz
66MHz
75MHz
90MHz
100MHz
120MHz

CENTRAL PROCESSING UNIT

There are four types of 486 chips.

486SX
486DX
486DX2
486DX4

CPU TYPE

486SX

An SX chip does not have a built-in math coprocessor.

486DX

A DX chip is the same as an SX chip, except it has a built-in math coprocessor. This makes a DX chip more expensive but faster at performing complex math calculations.

Math coprocessor
A math coprocessor assists the CPU by performing complex mathematical calculations. It can speed up your computer when you are working with graphics, scientific applications or math-intensive spreadsheets.

A math coprocessor is also called a floating point coprocessor or floating point unit.

Note: All Pentium chips have a built-in math coprocessor.

- Memory
- **Central Processing Unit**
- Memory Cache

CONSTRUCTING CPUs

Consider a U.S. road map printed on a fingernail and you can imagine the complexity of building a CPU chip. The elements in a CPU range from 0.35 to 1 micron. By comparison, a human hair is about 100 microns wide.

The manufacturing plants that produce CPUs, called fabrication facilities, are tens of thousands of times cleaner than hospital operating rooms. Ultra-sensitive dust filtering systems eliminate particles larger than 0.2 microns.

486DX2

A DX2 chip also has a built-in math coprocessor but processes and calculates information twice as fast as a DX chip. This improves the overall computer performance by up to 1.7 times.

486DX4

A DX4 chip also has a built-in math coprocessor but processes and calculates information three times as fast as a DX chip. This improves the overall computer performance by up to 2.5 times.

CENTRAL PROCESSING UNIT

UPGRADING A CPU

OVERDRIVE CPU

An OverDrive CPU replaces an existing CPU to increase the processing power of a computer. When you use an OverDrive CPU, you do not have to upgrade other parts of the computer to see an improvement in performance.

Note: Intel provides a booklet listing the computers that can use their OverDrive CPUs. This booklet should be available at stores selling OverDrive CPUs.

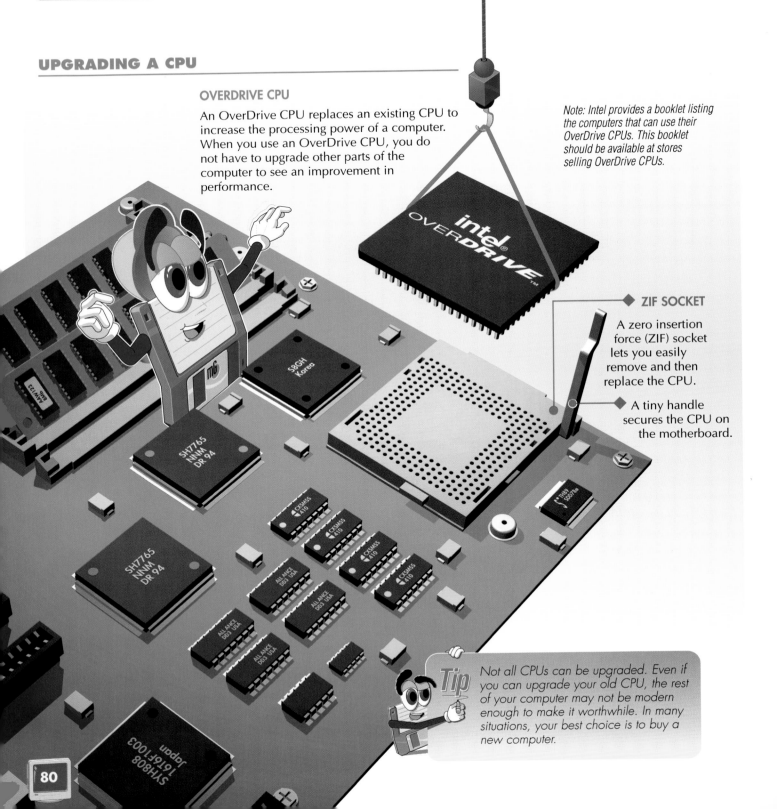

◆ ZIF SOCKET

A zero insertion force (ZIF) socket lets you easily remove and then replace the CPU.

◆ A tiny handle secures the CPU on the motherboard.

Tip

Not all CPUs can be upgraded. Even if you can upgrade your old CPU, the rest of your computer may not be modern enough to make it worthwhile. In many situations, your best choice is to buy a new computer.

CHOOSING A CPU

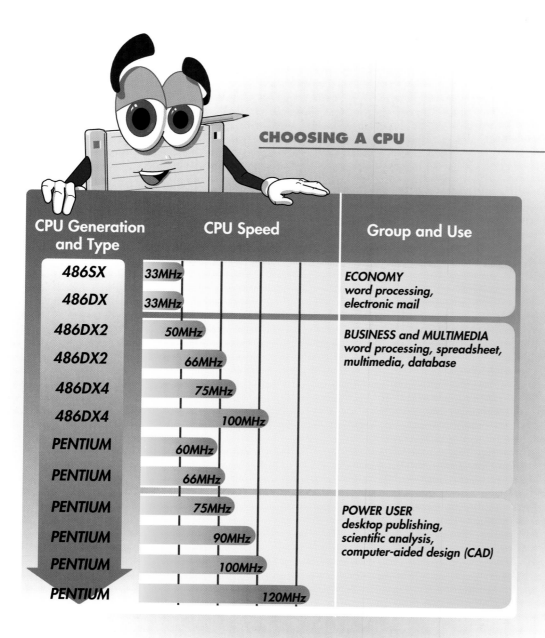

CPU Generation and Type	CPU Speed	Group and Use
486SX	33MHz	**ECONOMY** word processing, electronic mail
486DX	33MHz	
486DX2	50MHz	**BUSINESS and MULTIMEDIA** word processing, spreadsheet, multimedia, database
486DX2	66MHz	
486DX4	75MHz	
486DX4	100MHz	
PENTIUM	60MHz	
PENTIUM	66MHz	
PENTIUM	75MHz	**POWER USER** desktop publishing, scientific analysis, computer-aided design (CAD)
PENTIUM	90MHz	
PENTIUM	100MHz	
PENTIUM	120MHz	

As you move down the chart, CPU performance and cost both increase.

Your final decision should be based on your budget and intended use.

MEMORY CACHE

Memory cache reduces the time it takes the CPU to get information from the main memory. This speeds up the computer.

CPU

The CPU is the main chip that processes data in a computer. The CPU can get data from internal cache, external cache or main memory.

MAIN MEMORY (RAM)

If the CPU cannot find the data it needs in the external cache, it looks in the slower main memory, or RAM.

Each time the CPU requests data from the slower main memory, the computer places a copy of the data in the faster memory cache. This constantly updates the memory cache so it always contains the data most recently used by the CPU.

INTERNAL CACHE (L1)

Internal cache, or primary cache, consists of ultra-fast memory chips built into the CPU. These chips store a small amount of data recently used by the CPU.

When the CPU needs data, it first looks in the internal cache. Internal cache provides the fastest way for the CPU to get data.

EXTERNAL CACHE (L2)

External cache, or secondary cache, resides on the motherboard and consists of super-fast SRAM chips. These chips store data recently used by the CPU.

If the CPU cannot find the data it needs in the internal cache, it looks in the external cache. External cache is slower than internal cache but much faster than main memory.

Memory cache is similar to working with documents in your office.

1 When you need information, you first look through the documents on your desk (internal cache). This is the fastest way to get information.

2 If the information you need is not on your desk, you next look through the documents in your desk drawer (external cache). Getting this information takes time and slows down your work.

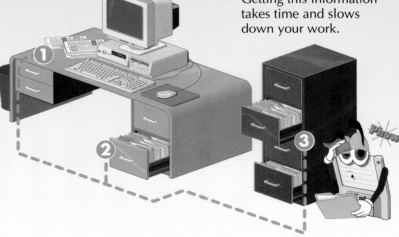

3 If the information you need is not in your desk drawer, you look in the filing cabinet (main memory). This slows down your work dramatically.

Note: Working without memory cache would be similar to going to the filing cabinet each time you need a document.

In this chapter you will learn about the devices a computer uses to store information.

STORAGE

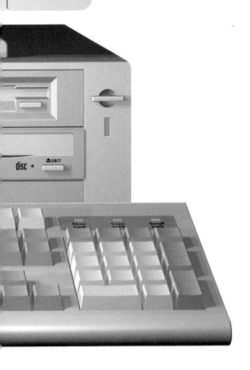

- Hard Drive
- Disk Cache
- Floppy Drive
- CD-ROM Drive
- Tape Drive

Hard Drive

HARD DRIVE

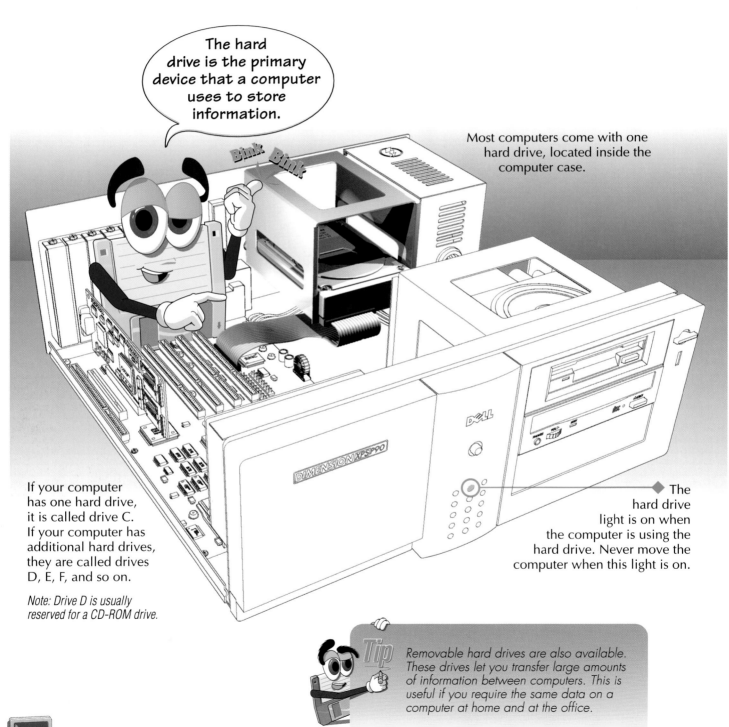

The hard drive is the primary device that a computer uses to store information.

Most computers come with one hard drive, located inside the computer case.

If your computer has one hard drive, it is called drive C. If your computer has additional hard drives, they are called drives D, E, F, and so on.

Note: Drive D is usually reserved for a CD-ROM drive.

◆ The hard drive light is on when the computer is using the hard drive. Never move the computer when this light is on.

Removable hard drives are also available. These drives let you transfer large amounts of information between computers. This is useful if you require the same data on a computer at home and at the office.

- **Hard Drive**
- Disk Cache
- Floppy Drive
- CD-ROM Drive
- Tape Drive

> The hard drive magnetically stores data on a stack of rotating disks called platters.

◆ Each disk has a read/write head that reads and records data on the disk.

HARD DRIVE CAPACITY AND SPEED

CAPACITY

The amount of information a hard drive can store is measured in bytes.

Purchase the largest hard drive you can afford. New programs and data will quickly fill a hard drive.

HOME AND BUSINESS

420MB to 1GB

POWER USERS

1GB (1,000MB) or higher

Note: 1MB equals approximately one novel.

SPEED

The speed that a hard drive finds data is called the average access time. Speed is measured in milliseconds (ms) and ranges from 10ms to 19ms for most hard drives. The lower the number, the faster the hard drive.

Note: 1 millisecond equals 1/1000 second.

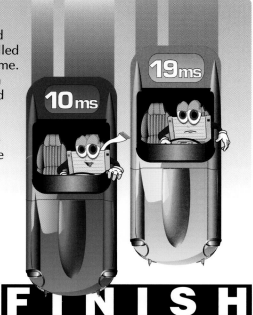

There are several ways to connect hard drives to a computer.

IDE

Integrated Drive Electronics (IDE) is the least expensive way of connecting a hard drive to a computer.

IDE can connect up to two hard drives to a computer. Each drive cannot store more than 528MB of data.

SCSI

Small Computer System Interface (SCSI, pronounced "scuzzy") is a fast and flexible, although expensive way of connecting a hard drive to a computer. It can also connect other devices such as CD-ROM drives, tape drives, scanners and printers. High-end computers and network servers come with SCSI.

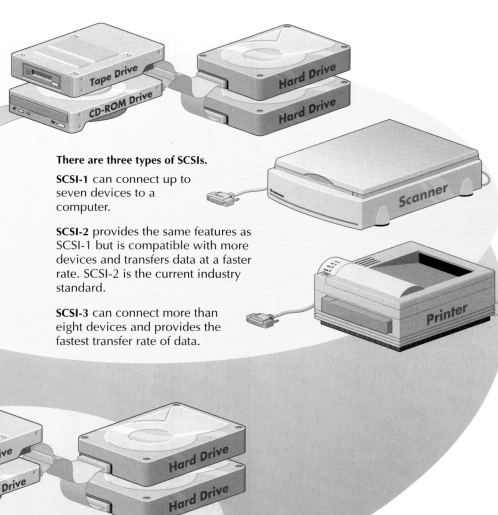

There are three types of SCSIs.

SCSI-1 can connect up to seven devices to a computer.

SCSI-2 provides the same features as SCSI-1 but is compatible with more devices and transfers data at a faster rate. SCSI-2 is the current industry standard.

SCSI-3 can connect more than eight devices and provides the fastest transfer rate of data.

EIDE

Enhanced IDE (EIDE) is faster and can connect more devices than IDE. Most new computers come with EIDE.

EIDE can connect up to four devices to a computer. These devices include hard drives, as well as CD-ROM and tape drives. Each hard drive can store more than 528MB of data.

HARD DRIVE

PROTECT A HARD DRIVE

ANTI-VIRUS PROGRAMS

A virus is a program that disrupts the normal operation of a computer. A virus can cause a variety of problems, such as the appearance of annoying messages on the screen or the destruction of information on the hard drive.

There are several ways that a virus can infect your computer:

- Viruses can attach themselves to data sent through a modem.

- Viruses can hide inside programs stored on floppy disks. They can also exist on floppy disks that do not contain files.

- Viruses can quickly spread through a computer network.

Follow these steps to protect a computer from viruses:

- Use an anti-virus program regularly to remove any viruses from your computer.

- If you receive files through a modem, immediately use an anti-virus program to check for viruses.

- Before using a colleague's floppy disk, check the disk for viruses.

- Remove all floppy disks before turning on your computer.

New viruses are created every day. To protect your computer, periodically update your anti-virus programs.

Note: MS-DOS versions 6.0 and 6.2 include anti-virus programs. You can also buy anti-virus programs at most computer stores.

BACK UP DATA

You should copy the data stored on your hard drive to floppy disks or tape cartridges. This provides you with extra copies in case viruses, theft or computer failure affect the original data. Back up your data at least once a day.

BACKUP DEVICES

Use floppy disks to back up less than 10MB of data.

Note: 1MB equals approximately one novel.

Use tape cartridges to back up more than 10MB of data. A single tape cartridge can store all the work from your hard drive (example: 120MB).

Note: To use a tape cartridge, you must have a tape drive.

Note: Windows 95 and MS-DOS versions 6.0 and 6.2 include backup programs. These programs help you copy data stored on your hard drive to floppy disks or tape cartridges.

HARD DRIVE

OPTIMIZE A HARD DRIVE

There are several ways that you can optimize the performance of a hard drive.

DISK DEFRAGMENTATION

A fragmented hard drive stores parts of a file in many different locations on a disk. To retrieve a file, the computer must search many areas on the disk.

You can use a defragmentation program to place all the parts of a file in one location. This reduces the time the hard drive will spend locating the file.

You should defragment your hard drive at least once a month to improve its performance.

Note: Windows 95 and MS-DOS versions 6.0 and 6.2 include a disk defragmentation program called Defragmenter.

STORAGE

- **Hard Drive**
- Disk Cache
- Floppy Drive
- CD-ROM Drive
- Tape Drive

DISK COMPRESSION

You can compress or squeeze together the files stored on a hard drive. This can double the storage capacity of the hard drive.

You should only compress your hard drive if it is running out of space to store new files.

Note: Windows 95 and MS-DOS versions 6.0 and 6.2 include a disk compression program called DriveSpace or DoubleSpace.

DISK REPAIR

You should use a disk repair program at least once a month to find and repair any hard drive problems.

Note: MS-DOS version 6.0 and earlier versions include a disk repair program called CHKDSK (check disk). MS-DOS version 6.2 and Windows 95 include a disk repair program called ScanDisk.

DISK CACHE

The disk cache reduces the time it takes the CPU to get information from the hard drive. This speeds up the computer.

CPU

The CPU is the main chip that processes data in a computer. The CPU can get data from the disk cache or from the hard drive.

HARD DRIVE

If the CPU cannot find the data it needs in the disk cache, it must get the data from the slower hard drive.

Each time the CPU requests data from the slower hard drive, the computer places a copy of the data in the faster disk cache. This constantly updates the disk cache so it always contains the most recently used data.

DISK CACHE

The disk cache is part of the computer's main memory that is set aside to store data recently used by the CPU.

When the CPU needs data, it first looks in the disk cache. The disk cache can supply data thousands of times faster than the hard drive.

Note: Most operating systems include software that automatically sets up the disk cache for you.

FLOPPY DRIVE

A floppy drive stores and retrieves information on floppy disks.

FLOPPY DISK

A floppy disk (or diskette) is a removable device that magnetically stores data.

If your computer has only one floppy drive, it is called **drive A**.

If your computer has two floppy drives, the second drive is called **drive B**.

- Hard Drive
- Disk Cache
- **Floppy Drive**
- CD-ROM Drive
- Tape Drive

FLOPPY DISK APPLICATIONS

TRANSFER DATA

You can use floppy disks to transfer data from one computer to another.

INSTALL NEW PROGRAMS

When you buy a program, it usually comes on several floppy disks. To use the program, you must copy the information stored on the disks to your computer.

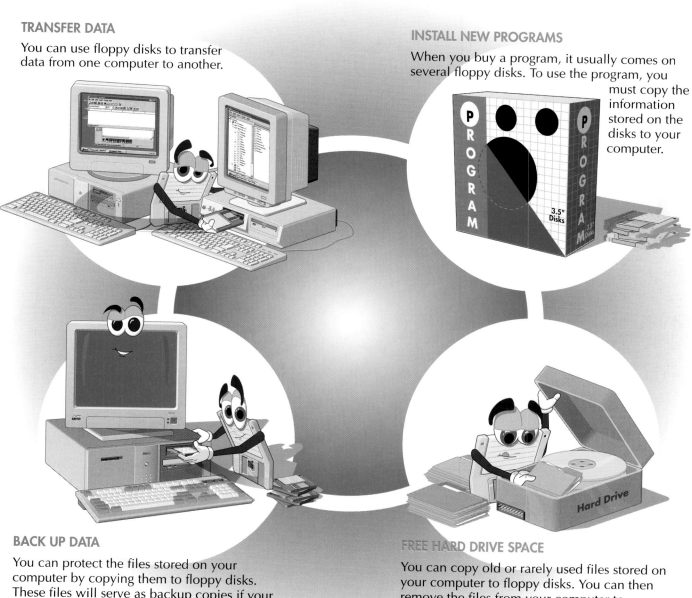

BACK UP DATA

You can protect the files stored on your computer by copying them to floppy disks. These files will serve as backup copies if your hard drive fails or if you accidentally erase important files.

FREE HARD DRIVE SPACE

You can copy old or rarely used files stored on your computer to floppy disks. You can then remove the files from your computer to provide more storage space.

FLOPPY DRIVE

5.25 INCH FLOPPY DISKS

◆ Most floppy disks provide a label so you can describe their contents. Use a soft-tipped felt marker to write on the label. A pen or pencil may damage the disk.

◆ You can prevent erasing and recording information on a 5.25 inch floppy disk by placing a small sticker over the write-protect notch.

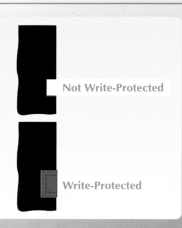

Not Write-Protected

Write-Protected

INSERTING A 5.25 INCH FLOPPY DISK

◆ This light is on when the drive is using the floppy disk. Never remove a floppy disk when this light is on.

2 Move the door latch down to secure the floppy disk.

◆ To remove the floppy disk, move the door latch to the horizontal position and then pull out the disk.

1 Push the floppy disk gently into the drive, label side up.

STORAGE

- Hard Drive
- Disk Cache
- **Floppy Drive**
- CD-ROM Drive
- Tape Drive

3.5 INCH FLOPPY DISKS

◆ You can prevent erasing and recording information on a 3.5 inch floppy disk by moving the tab to the write-protected position.

◆ Most floppy disks provide a label so you can describe their contents.

 Not Write-Protected

 Write-Protected

INSERTING A 3.5 INCH FLOPPY DISK

1 Push the floppy disk gently into the drive, label side up.

◆ Most drives make a clicking sound when you have fully inserted the floppy disk.

◆ To remove the floppy disk, press this button.

◆ This light is on when the drive is using the floppy disk. Never remove a floppy disk when this light is on.

FLOPPY DISK CAPACITY

Floppy disks come in two storage capacities. High-density disks store more information than double-density disks.

> The capacity of a floppy disk tells you how much information it can store.

**DOUBLE-DENSITY
720K**

720 PAGES

MicroFLOPPY
Double Sided
720 K

**HIGH-DENSITY
1.44MB**

1,440 PAGES

MicroFLOPPY
Double Sided
1.44 MB

◆ A double-density disk has only one hole at the top of the disk. It can store approximately 720 pages of double spaced text.

◆ A high-density disk has two holes at the top of the disk and usually displays the HD symbol. It can store approximately 1,440 pages of double spaced text.

**DOUBLE-DENSITY
360K**

360 PAGES

Double-Density   360 K

**HIGH-DENSITY
1.2MB**

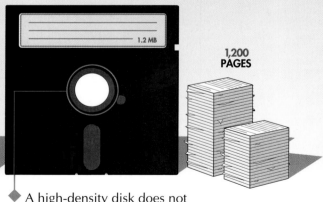

1.2 MB

1,200 PAGES

◆ A double-density disk has plastic around the center of the disk and is usually labeled. It can store approximately 360 pages of double spaced text.

◆ A high-density disk does not have plastic around the center of the disk. It can store approximately 1,200 pages of double spaced text.

STORAGE

- Hard Drive
- Disk Cache
- **Floppy Drive**
- CD-ROM Drive
- Tape Drive

FORMAT A FLOPPY DISK

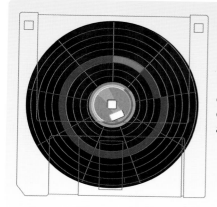

You must format a floppy disk before using it to store data.

Formatting prepares a floppy disk for use by dividing it into tracks and sectors. This organizes the disk so the computer can easily store and find information.

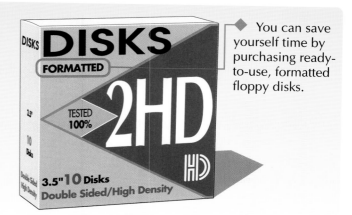

You can save yourself time by purchasing ready-to-use, formatted floppy disks.

PROTECT YOUR FLOPPY DISKS

- Keep floppy disks away from magnets, which can damage the information stored on the disks.

- Be careful not to spill liquids such as coffee or soda on floppy disks.

- Do not store floppy disks in extremely hot or cold locations.

CD-ROM DRIVE

Most CD-ROM drives are located inside the computer case. External units that connect to the computer by a cable are also available.

PHONES   VOL ▶   BUSY   disc ●   ⏏ EJECT

◆ To insert or remove a disc, press this button.

◆ This jack lets you listen to recorded sounds on a disc through headphones. Headphones are useful in noisy environments or when you want to listen to a disc privately.

◆ This light is on when the drive is using the disc. Never move the computer when this light is on.

◆ The volume control lets you adjust the sound level.

- Hard Drive
- Disk Cache
- Floppy Drive
- • **CD-ROM Drive**
- Tape Drive

A CD-ROM drive is a device that reads information stored on compact discs.

A single CD-ROM disc can store more than 600MB of data. This is equivalent to one set of encyclopedias.

The large storage capacity of a CD-ROM disc lets you conveniently install new programs on your computer. A program that needs twenty floppy disks to install can easily fit on a single CD-ROM disc.

Note: CD-ROM stands for Compact Disc - Read Only Memory.

CD-ROM DISC

A CD-ROM disc is the same type of disc that you buy at a music store.

CD-ROM discs store multimedia titles. Multimedia combines text, graphics, photographs, sound, animation and video to provide a powerful way of communicating information.

Note: You cannot change information stored on a CD-ROM disc.

Tip

CD-Recordable (CD-R) systems are available that let you store your own information on a disc. These systems are most commonly used for archiving information.

CD-ROM DRIVE

When buying a CD-ROM drive, you must consider three factors.

SPEED

The speed of a CD-ROM drive determines how fast the drive can transfer information from a disc to the computer. A faster speed results in better performance.

Note: The speed of a CD-ROM drive is also called the data transfer rate.

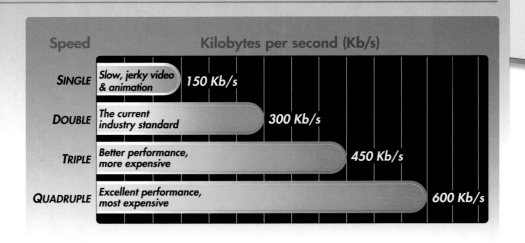

Speed	Kilobytes per second (Kb/s)	
SINGLE	Slow, jerky video & animation	150 Kb/s
DOUBLE	The current industry standard	300 Kb/s
TRIPLE	Better performance, more expensive	450 Kb/s
QUADRUPLE	Excellent performance, most expensive	600 Kb/s

- Hard Drive
- Disk Cache
- Floppy Drive
- CD-ROM Drive
- Tape Drive

AVERAGE ACCESS TIME

The average access time is the average time it takes a CD-ROM drive to find data stored on a disc. A lower access time results in better performance.

A CD-ROM drive should have an access time of less than 400ms, although an access time of 280ms or less is recommended.

SINGLE-SESSION OR MULTI-SESSION

Kodak introduced the Photo CD, which can store up to one hundred 35mm slides or negatives on a CD-ROM disc. If one set of slides does not completely fill a disc, you can have a photo finisher add more slides to the disc at a later date.

Single-session CD-ROM drives can only read the first set of slides stored on a disc. Multi-session drives are more expensive, but they can read the original and all slides later added to the disc.

TAPE DRIVE

A tape drive is a device that lets you copy the files stored on your computer to tape cartridges.

◆ A tape drive can be inside the computer case or connected to the computer by a cable.

External tape drives are more expensive, but you can use them with more than one computer.

◆ A tape drive stores data on tape cartridges. These cartridges are similar to the cassettes you buy at music stores.

Note: Tape drives are also called tape backup units.

- Hard Drive
- Disk Cache
- Floppy Drive
- CD-ROM Drive
- **Tape Drive**

TAPE DRIVE APPLICATIONS

BACK UP DATA

You can protect the files stored on your computer by copying them to a tape cartridge. This provides you with extra copies in case viruses, theft or computer failure affect the original files.

ARCHIVE DATA

You can copy old or rarely used files on your computer to tape cartridges. You can then remove the files from your hard drive to provide more storage space.

BACKUP PROGRAM

A backup program helps you copy the data stored on your computer to tape cartridges.

You can set a backup program to run automatically. This lets you schedule a backup at night, when you are not using your computer.

You can set a backup program to copy all the files on your hard drive, specific files or only files that recently changed.

Note: Windows 95 and MS-DOS versions 6.0 and 6.2 include backup programs.

TAPE DRIVE

QIC DRIVE

A quarter-inch cartridge (QIC) drive is ideal for backing up information stored on a single computer.

You can use a QIC drive or a DAT drive to back up information stored on your computer.

QIC minicartridges are available in several storage capacities. The QIC-80 minicartridge is currently the most popular.

Note: QIC cartridges also come in a larger, less popular size. These full-size cartridges are more expensive, but they can store more information.

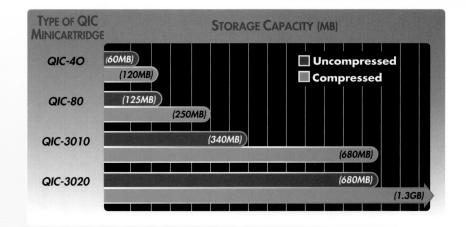

TYPE OF QIC MINICARTRIDGE	STORAGE CAPACITY (MB)
QIC-40	(60MB) / (120MB)
QIC-80	(125MB) / (250MB)
QIC-3010	(340MB) / (680MB)
QIC-3020	(680MB) / (1.3GB)

☐ Uncompressed
☐ Compressed

You can double the amount of data stored on a tape cartridge by compressing the data. For example, a 125MB tape can store 250MB of compressed data.

STORAGE

- Hard Drive
- Disk Cache
- Floppy Drive
- CD-ROM Drive
- Tape Drive

DAT DRIVE

A digital audio tape (DAT) drive is ideal for backing up information stored on a server. A server stores the files of everyone connected to a network.

DAT drives are faster but more expensive than QIC drives. DAT cartridges generally store more information than QIC minicartridges.

When buying a DAT drive, make sure it follows the DDS-2 standard. This standard doubles the storage capacity of the older DDS-1 drives from 2GB to 4GB.

BACKUP STRATEGIES

Back up your work frequently. Consider how much work you can afford to lose. If you can afford to lose the work accomplished in one day, back up once a day. If your files do not often change during the week, back up once a week.

Create and then strictly follow a backup schedule. Hard drive disasters always seem to happen right after you miss a scheduled backup.

Store all of your cassettes in a cool, dry place, away from electrical equipment.

Minimize your chances of losing important data by making at least two sets of backup copies. Keep one set near your computer and the second set in another building.

In this chapter you will learn how multimedia can inform and entertain you. You will also learn what features your computer needs to get the most from multimedia.

World of Music - North America
North American Jazz

Select Advance Back Up Play Pause Capture Quit

The Bass Player

The bass player is one of the most important players in any jazz band, whose importance increases as the number of players decreases. Without a drummer, the band must rely on the rhythm of their bassist to keep the group in time and to provide the low end sound that accents the higher octave instruments like the piano and trumpet.

Audio Text Help

o hear trio samples

MULTIMEDIA

INTRODUCTION TO MULTIMEDIA

Multimedia is an exciting mix of graphics, text, video, sound, animation and photographs.

World of Music - North America
North American Jazz

| Select | Advance | Back Up | Play | Pause | Capture | Quit |

The Bass Player

The bass player is one of the most important players in any jazz band, whose importance increases as the number of players decreases. Without a drummer, the band must rely on the rhythm of their bassist to keep the group in time and to provide the low end sound that accents the higher octave instruments like the piano and trumpet.

Audio Text   Help

...to hear trio samples

GRAPHICS

Multimedia titles let you see full-color graphics on your screen. You can often select a graphic to produce sound effects or display related information.

TEXT

A single CD-ROM disc can store the information from an entire set of encyclopedias. Multimedia packages let you search for text on any topic and see the results in seconds. Once you find a topic of interest, you can instantly jump to a related topic by selecting specially marked text, called **hypertext**.

VIDEO

You can watch a video on your computer screen. Just like a VCR, you can slow down or speed up the video.

SOUND

You can listen to music and sound effects while using a multimedia title. This can make a topic more interesting and meaningful. For example, you can listen to a dinosaur roar, a space flight launch or Beethoven's Ninth Symphony. Just like a stereo, you can turn up the volume and repeat your favorite selections.

ANIMATION

You can watch colorful animations that show you how things work. An animation can take you through a battle, the solar system or the development of a plant. You can replay an animation as often as you like.

PHOTOGRAPHS

You can view full-color photographs on your screen. You can then print your favorite photographs on a black and white or color printer.

113

There are thousands of multimedia titles available to inform and entertain you.

You can buy multimedia titles in stores that supply software, office supplies and books. Most CD-ROM discs cost between $30 and $100.

CHILDREN

Hundreds of multimedia titles are available to stimulate a child's imagination. There are stories that offer magical adventures and games for children of all ages. Many games teach basic skills such as reading, writing, spelling and math.

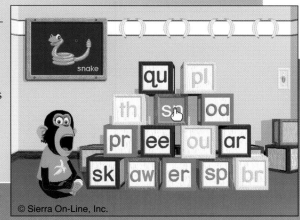
© Sierra On-Line, Inc.

HISTORY AND POLITICS

Numerous multimedia titles let you watch, listen and learn about recent events and explore ancient civilizations. You can learn about prehistoric life, the JFK assassination or Clinton's campaign for presidency.

EDUCATION

There are many stimulating and comprehensive educational titles that can teach you new skills. You can learn how to type, use a computer or speak a new language.

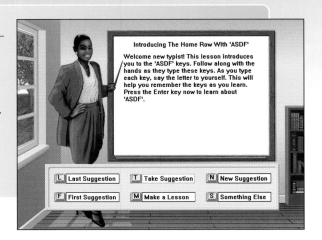

MULTIMEDIA TITLES

THE ARTS

You can examine art, music and literature through multimedia packages. You can stroll through an art gallery or an exotic garden, learn about the instruments in an orchestra or read Shakespearean plays.

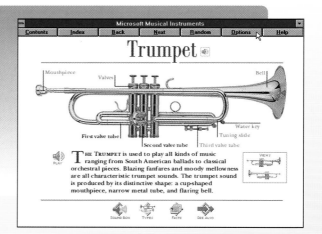

Multimedia titles provide a powerful way of communicating information.

HEALTH AND SCIENCE

You can learn about the exciting world of health and science. You can learn yoga, discover how to cure common illnesses, explore the solar system, learn about the human body or examine the world of bugs.

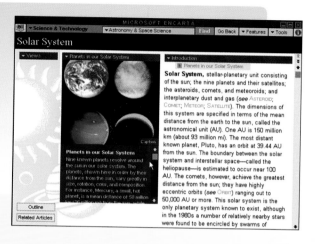

GAMES

Multimedia games can keep you entertained for hours. You can defend your world from invading aliens, play golf or football, try to defeat the dealer in a blackjack game or enjoy the sights and sounds of real flight.

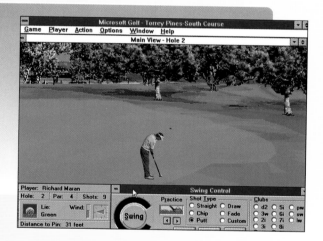

REFERENCE

CD-ROM discs provide an excellent source of information. A single CD-ROM disc can store the information from an entire set of encyclopedias, complete with drawings, photographs, video and sound. You can also buy maps, magazine articles, phone books and dictionaries on CD-ROM discs.

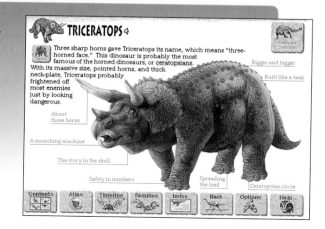

MULTIMEDIA COMPUTER SYSTEMS

The multimedia personal computer (MPC) marketing council has listed the requirements for a multimedia computer system. Products certified by this council display the MPC2 symbol.

Note: MPC2 replaced the original MPC1 guidelines, which are now obsolete.

CD-ROM DRIVE

A CD-ROM drive reads information stored on compact discs.

Minimum:
Double-speed (300Kb/s)
400ms access time
Multi-session

Recommended:
Double-speed (300Kb/s)
280ms or less access time
Multi-session

Note: For more information on CD-ROM drives, refer to pages 102 to 105.

HARD DRIVE

The hard drive is the primary device that a computer uses to store information.

Minimum: 160MB
Recommended: 540MB

Note: For more information on hard drives, refer to pages 86 to 93.

CPU

The central processing unit (CPU) is the main chip in a computer. It processes instructions and performs calculations.

Minimum: 25MHz 486SX

Recommended: 66MHz 486DX2 or better

Note: For more information on CPUs, refer to pages 74 to 81.

RAM

RAM temporarily stores data inside a computer.

Minimum: 4MB

Recommended: 8MB

Note: For more information on RAM, refer to pages 70 to 73.

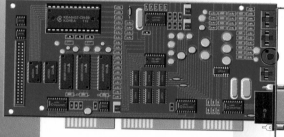

SOUND CARD

A sound card improves the sound quality of a computer.

Recommended: 16-bit

Note: For more information on sound cards, refer to pages 64 to 67.

VIDEO ADAPTER

The video adapter generates the images displayed on the screen.

Minimum:
256 colors (8-bit color)

Recommended:
65,536 colors (16-bit color)

Note: For more information on video adapters, refer to pages 34 to 43.

eller 2100

PORTABLE COMPUTERS

A portable computer has a built-in keyboard and screen. This eliminates the need for cables to connect these devices.

PORTABLE COMPUTERS

• **Introduction**   • Input and Output Devices
• Batteries   • Storage Devices
• Screens   • Processing
• PC Cards   • Connections

ADVANTAGES OF PORTABLES

A portable computer lets you work while traveling on a plane or train. It also lets you bring work home rather than stay late at the office.

You can easily bring a portable computer to meetings to present information.

TYPES OF PORTABLES

NOTEBOOK

A notebook weighs between six and eight pounds and is the size of a three-ring binder. A notebook can perform the same functions as all but the high-end desktop computers.

SUBNOTEBOOK

A subnotebook weighs between two and six pounds. Subnotebooks have less power, less storage space and smaller screens than notebooks. This type of portable is ideal for frequent travelers because of its light weight.

PALMTOP

A palmtop is a hand-held device that weighs less than one pound. This type of portable is most often used as a daily organizer.

*Note: A **laptop** is a portable computer that weighs between eight and ten pounds. Laptops are now obsolete, since lighter, full-featured notebook computers are widely available.*

BATTERIES

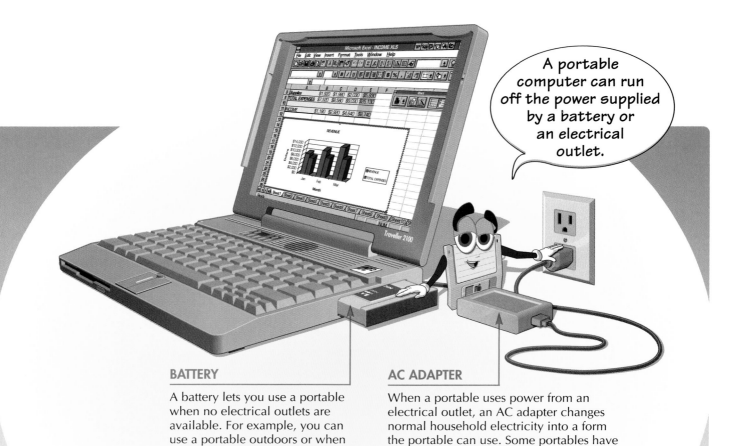

A portable computer can run off the power supplied by a battery or an electrical outlet.

BATTERY

A battery lets you use a portable when no electrical outlets are available. For example, you can use a portable outdoors or when traveling.

AC ADAPTER

When a portable uses power from an electrical outlet, an AC adapter changes normal household electricity into a form the portable can use. Some portables have an AC adapter built into the computer case.

RECHARGING BATTERIES

A battery lasts for only a few hours. You must recharge a battery to use it again. If you are unable to recharge a battery when traveling, bring an extra battery so you can work for a longer period of time.

MONITORING BATTERIES

Most portables display the amount of battery life remaining either on the screen or on a panel built into the computer.

PORTABLE COMPUTERS

- Introduction
- **Batteries**
- Screens
- PC Cards
- Input and Output Devices
- Storage Devices
- Processing
- Connections

TYPES OF BATTERIES

NICKEL CADMIUM (NiCd)

Battery life: 1 to 2 hours

NiCd batteries are the oldest and least expensive type of battery. NiCd batteries suffer from memory effects. This means you must completely drain the battery before recharging it to get the maximum charge.

The cadmium (Cd) in NiCd batteries is highly toxic. Contact your local waste management office for information on battery disposal.

NICKEL METAL HYDRIDE (NiMH)

Battery life: 2 to 3 hours

NiMH batteries have almost completely replaced NiCd batteries. NiMH batteries are more expensive but less toxic, less prone to memory effects and longer-lasting than NiCd batteries.

LITHIUM-ION

Battery life: 4 to 5 hours

Lithium-ion batteries are the longest-lasting but most expensive type of battery. They do not suffer from memory effects, but they take longer to recharge than NiMH batteries.

The screens on portables use liquid crystal displays (LCDs). This is the same type of display used in most digital wristwatches.

LCD

LCD screens use very little electricity and weigh much less than the screens on desktop computers. This prolongs battery life and makes portables easier to carry.

BACKLIGHTING

Most portables have an internal light source at the back or side of the screen. This makes the screen easier to view in low-light areas but shortens battery life.

BUYING TIPS

• The screen should measure at least 9 inches diagonally.

• The screen should display at least 256 colors at 640 x 480 resolution.

• Make sure the portable has a socket for connecting an external monitor.

• If you are using a portable for presentations, make sure it can operate both your portable and an external monitor at the same time.

PORTABLE COMPUTERS

- Introduction
- Batteries
- Screens
- PC Cards
- Input and Output Devices
- Storage Devices
- Processing
- Connections

TYPES OF SCREENS

MONOCHROME PASSIVE MATRIX

This type of screen can only display shades of gray. Monochrome passive matrix screens are becoming obsolete, since they are close in price to color passive matrix screens.

COLOR PASSIVE MATRIX

This type of screen is not as bright or as rich in color as an active matrix screen, but is much less expensive. The lower cost makes it ideal for routine office tasks.

Passive matrix screens are difficult to read when viewed from an angle. This is ideal when you want to keep work private from people sitting next to you on a train or plane, but makes delivering presentations to several people difficult.

Always buy dual-scan passive matrix screens. Beware of inexpensive single-scan passive matrix screens that make colors look pale and washed out.

Note: Passive matrix screens are also called Super Twist Nematic (STN) screens.

COLOR ACTIVE MATRIX

This type of screen is more expensive than a passive matrix screen but displays brighter, richer colors.

You can view active matrix screens from wide angles. This is ideal for delivering presentations to several people.

Active matrix screens are ideal for business presentations and multimedia.

Note: Active matrix screens are also called Thin-Film Transistor (TFT) screens.

PC CARDS

A PC Card is a lightweight, credit card sized device that lets you add a new feature to a portable computer.

Adding new features to a portable adds weight and takes up valuable room. To solve these problems, the Personal Computer Memory Card International Association (PCMCIA) designed the PC Card to add new features to portable computers.

Note: A PC Card is also called a PCMCIA Card.

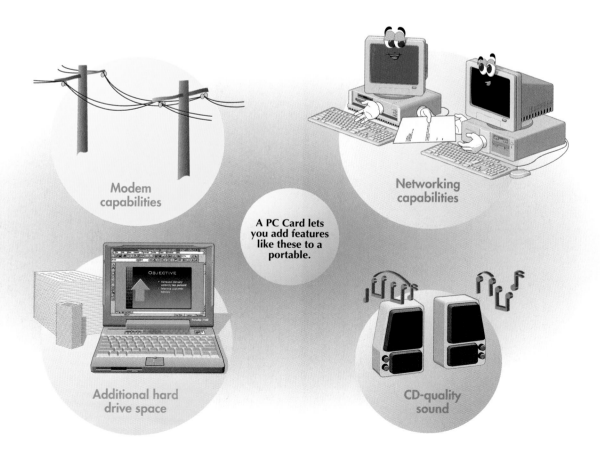

Modem capabilities

Networking capabilities

A PC Card lets you add features like these to a portable.

Additional hard drive space

CD-quality sound

You insert a PC Card into a PC slot.

Most portable computers have two slots that accept PC Cards. This lets you insert:

• two Type I cards, or
• two Type II cards, or
• one Type III card.

TYPES OF PC CARDS

TYPE I

3.3 mm thick

This PC Card is used to add memory to a portable.

TYPE II

5.0 mm thick

This PC Card is used to add modem capabilities, networking capabilities or CD-quality sound to a portable.

TYPE III

10.5 mm thick

This PC Card is used to add larger devices such as a removable hard drive to a portable.

Note: Some PC Cards contain multiple features. For example, a single PC Card can provide CD-quality sound and modem capabilities.

POINTING DEVICES

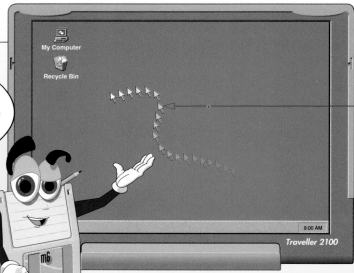

There are several devices that let you move the mouse pointer around the screen.

My Computer

Recycle Bin

Mouse pointer

Traveller 2100

POINTING STICK

Many portables have a small, eraser-like device that you push in different directions to move the mouse pointer on the screen.

TRACKBALL

A trackball is an upside-down mouse that remains stationary. You roll the ball with your fingers or palm to move the mouse pointer on the screen.

Trackballs that attach to the side of a portable can easily be knocked off. Look for built-in trackballs.

If you are left-handed, beware of trackballs placed on the right side of the keyboard.

TOUCHPAD

A touchpad is a pressure and motion sensitive surface. You move your fingertip around the touchpad to control the mouse pointer on the screen.

MOUSE

A mouse is a hand-held device. When you move the mouse on a flat surface, the mouse pointer on the screen moves in the same direction. A mouse is impractical when traveling, since you need a relatively large, flat surface to move the mouse.

KEYBOARD

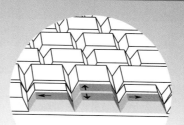

CURSOR KEYS

Make sure the cursor keys appear in an inverted T position. This is the best key arrangement for moving the mouse pointer on the screen.

The keys on a portable are small and close together to save space. Before buying a portable, make sure you type several paragraphs of text to make sure the keyboard is suitable for you.

MODEM

You can buy a portable with a built-in modem or add modem capabilities by inserting a PC Card. When traveling, a modem lets you communicate with your office through telephone lines. This is useful if you want to check your electronic messages or retrieve information from your office.

Note: The current passing through some hotel phone systems may damage a modem. Check with hotel management before plugging in your modem.

PORTABLE PRINTERS

You can buy tiny, battery-powered printers to output your work when traveling.

131

STORAGE DEVICES

HARD DRIVE

A hard drive is the primary device that a portable uses to store programs and data.

Buy the largest hard drive you can afford. New programs and data will quickly fill a hard drive. Most portables should have at least 200MB of storage space.

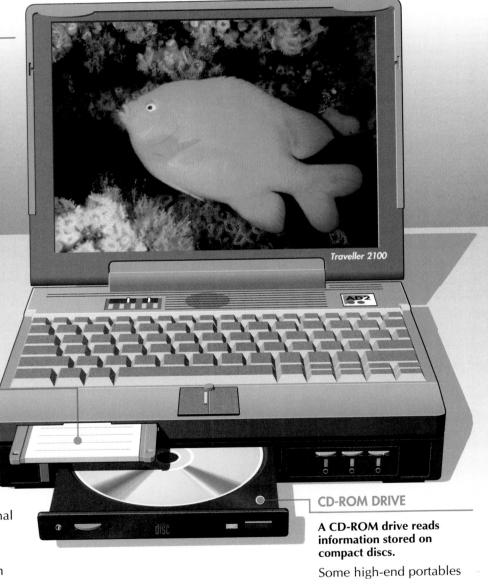

FLOPPY DRIVE

A floppy drive stores and retrieves information on floppy disks.

You can buy a portable without a floppy drive to reduce its weight. If you want to use a floppy drive, you can connect the portable to an external floppy drive.

Some portables let you remove a floppy drive and replace it with a second battery. This doubles the amount of time you can use the portable.

CD-ROM DRIVE

A CD-ROM drive reads information stored on compact discs.

Some high-end portables now come with CD-ROM drives. These portables are usually referred to as multimedia portables.

PORTABLE COMPUTERS

- Introduction
- Batteries
- Screens
- PC Cards
- Input and Output Devices
- Storage Devices
- Processing
- Connections

PROCESSING

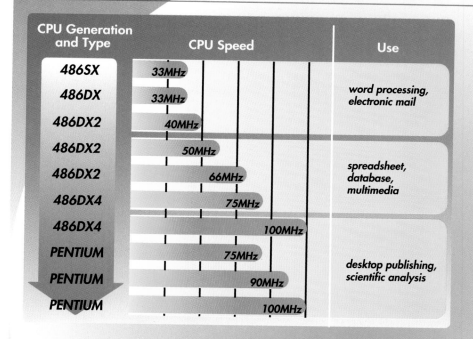

CPU Generation and Type	CPU Speed	Use
486SX	33MHz	word processing, electronic mail
486DX	33MHz	
486DX2	40MHz	
486DX2	50MHz	spreadsheet, database, multimedia
486DX2	66MHz	
486DX4	75MHz	
486DX4	100MHz	desktop publishing, scientific analysis
PENTIUM	75MHz	
PENTIUM	90MHz	
PENTIUM	100MHz	

CPU

The central processing unit (CPU) is the main chip in a portable. It performs calculations and processes instructions.

As you move down the chart, CPU performance and cost both increase. Your final decision should be based on your budget and intended use.

MEMORY

Memory (or RAM) temporarily stores data inside a portable. It works like a blackboard that is constantly overwritten with new data.

A portable needs at least 8MB of memory to ensure that programs run smoothly. More memory will also extend battery life.

$$3.14 \times (3a^2 \times 700) \div 1{,}298 - .654$$

CONNECTIONS

CONNECTING DEVICES TO A PORTABLE

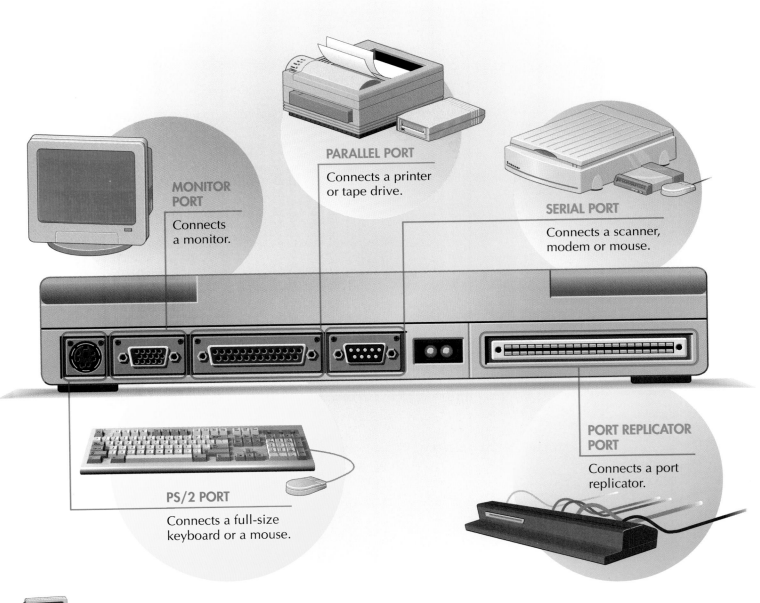

PARALLEL PORT
Connects a printer or tape drive.

MONITOR PORT
Connects a monitor.

SERIAL PORT
Connects a scanner, modem or mouse.

PS/2 PORT
Connects a full-size keyboard or a mouse.

PORT REPLICATOR PORT
Connects a port replicator.

134

PORTABLE COMPUTERS

- Introduction
- Batteries
- Screens
- PC Cards

- Input and Output Devices
- Storage Devices
- Processing
- **Connections**

USING YOUR PORTABLE AT WORK

PORT REPLICATOR

A port replicator lets you quickly connect devices to a portable.

A port replicator has the same ports as those found on the back of a portable. Devices such as a monitor, keyboard, modem and mouse plug into the port replicator.

A portable connects to the port replicator in one step. This lets the portable use all the devices attached to the port replicator without the cumbersome task of attaching each individual cable.

A port replicator is smaller, lighter and less expensive than a docking station.

DOCKING STATION

Like a port replicator, a docking station lets you quickly connect devices to a portable. It also extends the capabilities of a portable.

When you connect a portable to a docking station, the portable can use all the features found on the docking station, such as a CD-ROM drive, tape drive, network and modem.

The need for docking stations will eventually disappear, since PC Cards offer a simpler way of extending the capabilities of a computer.

In this chapter you will learn about operating systems and how they control the overall activity of computers.

OPERATING SYSTEMS

INTRODUCTION TO OPERATING SYSTEMS

An operating system is a program that controls the overall activity of a computer.

Like an orchestra conductor, an operating system ensures that all parts of your computer work together smoothly and efficiently.

CONTROLS YOUR HARDWARE

An operating system controls the different parts of a computer system, such as the printer and monitor, and enables them to work together.

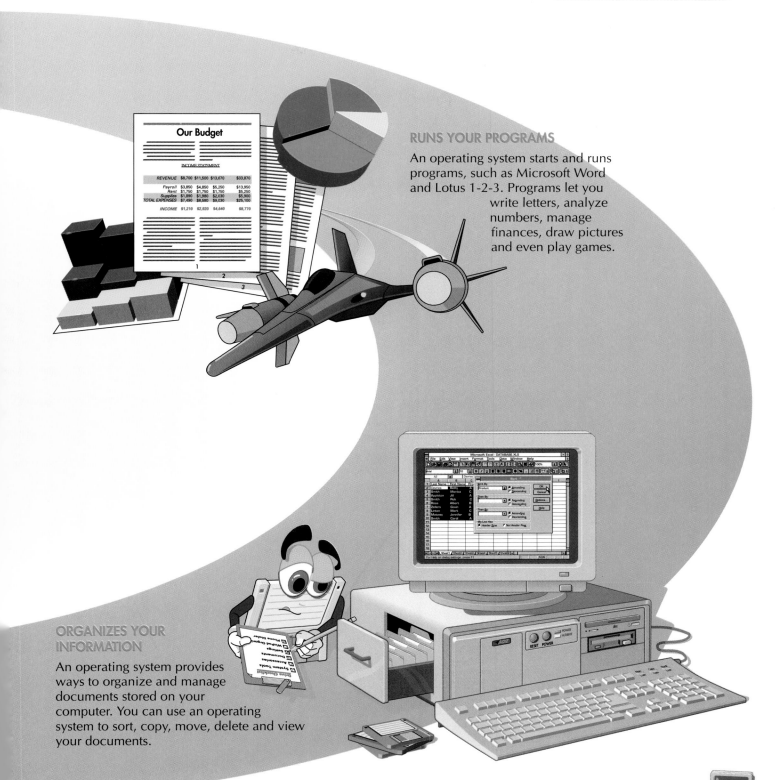

RUNS YOUR PROGRAMS

An operating system starts and runs programs, such as Microsoft Word and Lotus 1-2-3. Programs let you write letters, analyze numbers, manage finances, draw pictures and even play games.

ORGANIZES YOUR INFORMATION

An operating system provides ways to organize and manage documents stored on your computer. You can use an operating system to sort, copy, move, delete and view your documents.

MS-DOS

MS-DOS is an operating system that uses text commands you enter to perform tasks.

Note: MS-DOS stands for Microsoft Disk Operating System.

```
C:\> DIR\DATA\123DATA

Volume in drive C has no label
Volume Serial Number is 12FA-3823
Directory of C:\DATA\123DATA

.              <DIR>         03-10-95   2:43p
..             <DIR>         01-10-95   3:15p
INCOME1Q  WK4      10,005   04-08-95   9:01a
INCOME2Q  WK4      15,609   02-16-95   9:23a
INCOME3Q  WK4      12,444   03-10-95   4:20p
JIM       WK4      11,959   03-15-95   9:55a
PLAN1     WK4      13,999   01-08-95   1:40p
PLAN2     WK4      17,909   02-15-95   9:43a
PLAN3     WK4      11,555   04-20-95   8:54p
PROJECT1  WK4      12,202   01-17-95   2:04p
PROJECT2  WK4      15,898   02-15-95   2:20p
PROJECT3  WK4      19,345   02-08-95   9:09a
        12 file(s)        140,925 bytes
                       96,026,624 bytes free

C:\>
```

COMMAND PROMPT

Tells you that MS-DOS is ready to accept a command.

CURSOR

The flashing line on the screen. The cursor indicates where the text you type will appear.

COMMAND

You enter a command to perform a task or start a program.

A single command can usually tell the computer what you want to accomplish. For example, the DIR command tells the computer to list the subdirectories and files stored in a directory.

DIRECTORY

MS-DOS uses directories to organize the data stored on a computer.

FILENAME

You must name a file to store it on a computer.

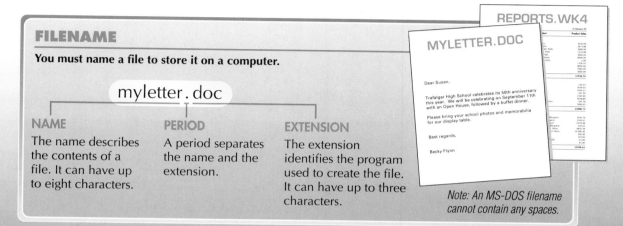

myletter.doc

NAME

The name describes the contents of a file. It can have up to eight characters.

PERIOD

A period separates the name and the extension.

EXTENSION

The extension identifies the program used to create the file. It can have up to three characters.

Note: An MS-DOS filename cannot contain any spaces.

REPORTS.WK4

MYLETTER.DOC

Dear Susan,

Trafalgar High School celebrates its 50th anniversary this year. We will be celebrating on September 11th with an Open House, followed by a buffet dinner.

Please bring your school photos and memorabilia for our display table.

Best regards,

Becky Flynn

UTILITIES

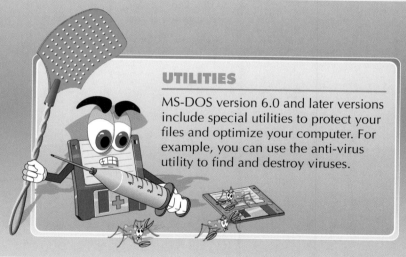

MS-DOS version 6.0 and later versions include special utilities to protect your files and optimize your computer. For example, you can use the anti-virus utility to find and destroy viruses.

MS-DOS SHELL

The MS-DOS Shell makes MS-DOS easier to use. The Shell provides a graphical display, which is far less intimidating than the lines of text displayed in MS-DOS.

You can use a mouse with the MS-DOS Shell.

Note: The MS-DOS Shell was first introduced in MS-DOS version 5.0.

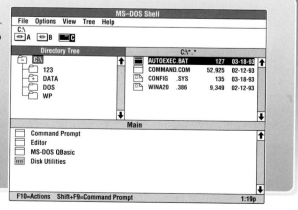

WINDOWS 3.1

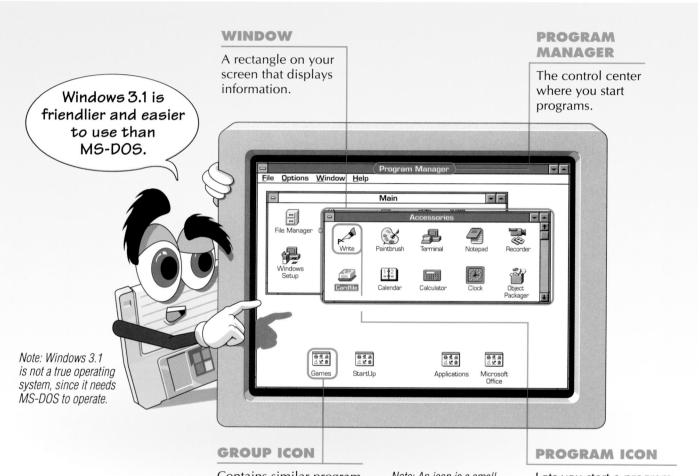

WINDOW

A rectangle on your screen that displays information.

PROGRAM MANAGER

The control center where you start programs.

Windows 3.1 is friendlier and easier to use than MS-DOS.

Note: Windows 3.1 is not a true operating system, since it needs MS-DOS to operate.

GROUP ICON

Contains similar program icons. For example, the Games group icon contains several games.

Note: An icon is a small picture on your screen that represents an object, such as a file or program.

PROGRAM ICON

Lets you start a program. Programs allow you to write letters, analyze numbers, create presentations and much more.

A mouse is essential when working with Windows.

142

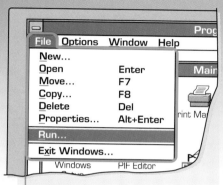

MENU

A menu lists related commands that let you accomplish tasks. For example, the Run command lets you start a program or open a document.

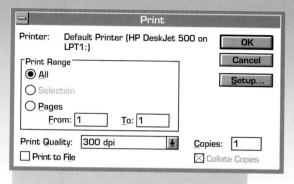

DIALOG BOX

A dialog box lets you select options before carrying out a command. For example, the Print dialog box lets you choose the pages you want to print.

WORK WITH MULTIPLE PROGRAMS

Windows 3.1 lets you run several programs at the same time. This lets you instantly switch between programs. For example, you can write a letter and then instantly switch to another program to check your sales figures.

• Most Windows programs look and act the same. Once you learn one program, you can quickly learn others.

• You can easily exchange information between programs.

Note: You can run MS-DOS programs while working in Windows 3.1.

WINDOWS 3.1

FILE MANAGER

The File Manager is a program in Windows 3.1 that lets you view and organize all the files stored on your computer. You can use the File Manager to sort, copy, move and delete files.

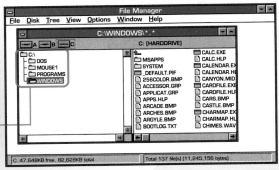

DIRECTORY

Windows 3.1 uses directories, or folders, to help organize the data stored on your computer.

ACCESSORIES

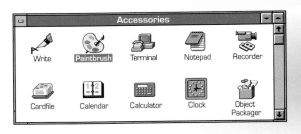

Windows 3.1 provides several accessories, or mini-programs, that let you accomplish simple tasks. For example, the Paintbrush program lets you draw pictures, maps and signs.

GAMES

Windows 3.1 provides a few simple games to entertain you. You can buy additional games at most computer stores.

CONTROL PANEL

The Control Panel lets you change the way Windows 3.1 looks and acts. You can change the date set in the computer, the colors displayed on the screen and much more.

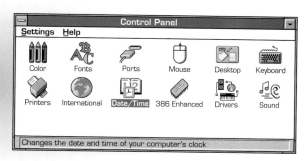

OTHER WINDOWS VERSIONS

WINDOWS FOR WORKGROUPS 3.11

Windows for Workgroups (WFW) 3.11 is a more powerful version of Windows 3.1. This program looks and acts like Windows 3.1 but operates faster, includes a few new applications and lets you exchange information through a network.

WINDOWS NT

Windows New Technology (NT) targets the top ten percent of computer users who need a powerful operating system. Unlike Windows 3.1 and Windows for Workgroups 3.11, this program is a true operating system because it does not need MS-DOS to operate.

Windows NT lets you exchange information through a network. It also provides security features to protect information and lets you use up to 255 characters to name a document.

WINDOWS 95

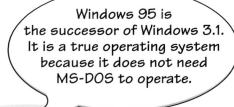

Windows 95 is the successor of Windows 3.1. It is a true operating system because it does not need MS-DOS to operate.

MY COMPUTER

Lets you view all the folders and documents stored on your computer.

RECYCLE BIN

Stores all the documents you delete and allows you to recover them later.

START BUTTON

Gives you quick access to programs and documents.

SHORTCUT

You can place a shortcut to a document on your screen. This lets you quickly open documents you use regularly.

TASKBAR

Displays the name of each open window on your screen. This lets you easily switch between the open windows.

Windows 95 is more graphical than Windows 3.1. This makes Windows 95 easier to use.

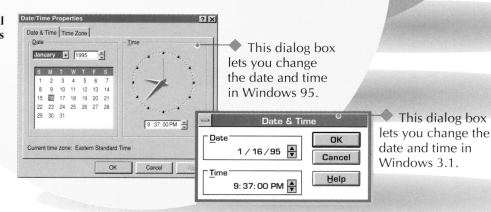

◆ This dialog box lets you change the date and time in Windows 95.

◆ This dialog box lets you change the date and time in Windows 3.1.

PLUG AND PLAY

Windows 95 supports Plug and Play technology. This technology lets you add new features to a computer without complex and time-consuming installation procedures.

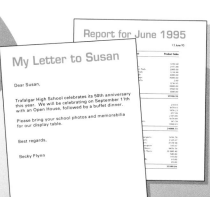

FILENAMES

Windows 95 lets you use up to 255 characters to name a document.

Note: Windows 3.1 filenames can be up to 8 characters long with a 3 character extension (example: myletter.doc).

EXPLORER

Like a road map, the Windows Explorer lets you view the location of each folder and document on your computer. You can use the Explorer to manage your information.

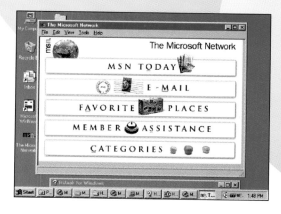

THE MICROSOFT NETWORK

Like CompuServe or Prodigy, The Microsoft Network is an on-line information service. It provides data from sources around the world and lets you communicate with other people connected to the service.

The Microsoft Network also lets you connect to the Internet. The Internet provides a vast amount of information, news and advice and now reaches over thirty million people.

In this chapter
you will learn about
application software.
Application software helps you
write letters, analyze numbers,
manage large collections of
information and
much more.

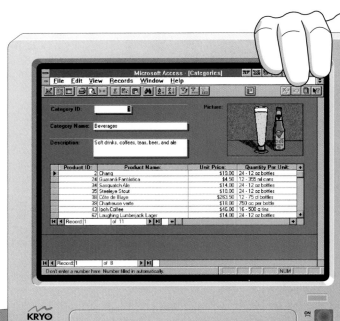

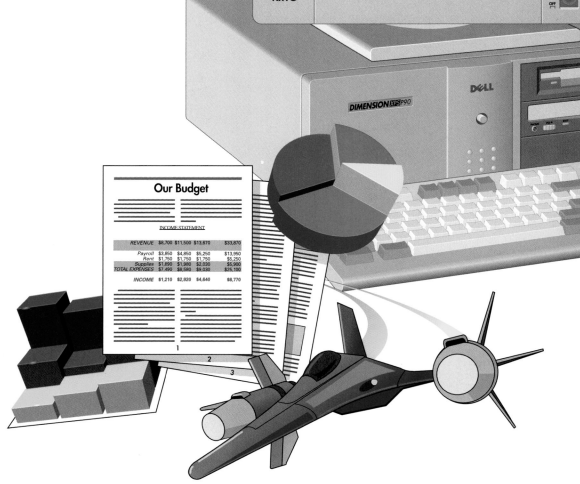

APPLICATION SOFTWARE

Word Processing

Spreadsheets

Databases

Desktop Publishing

Suites

WORD PROCESSING

A word processor lets you produce documents quickly and efficiently. You can take advantage of the editing and formatting features to produce professional-looking documents.

WHAT YOU CAN CREATE WITH A WORD PROCESSOR

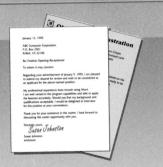

PERSONAL AND BUSINESS LETTERS

A word processor helps you produce letters quickly and accurately.

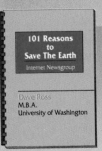

REPORTS AND MANUALS

A word processor provides editing and formatting features that make it easy to produce longer documents, such as reports and manuals.

NEWSLETTERS AND BROCHURES

You can use the formatting features and graphics provided by a word processor to produce attractive newsletters and brochures.

- **Word Processing**
- Spreadsheets
- Databases
- Desktop Publishing
- Suites

WORD PROCESSOR BASICS

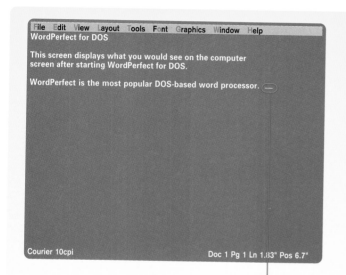

```
File  Edit  View  Layout  Tools  Font  Graphics  Window  Help
WordPerfect for DOS

This screen displays what you would see on the computer
screen after starting WordPerfect for DOS.

WordPerfect is the most popular DOS-based word processor.

Courier 10cpi                              Doc 1 Pg 1 Ln 1.83" Pos 6.7"
```

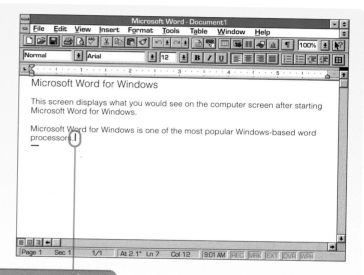

```
Microsoft Word - Document1
File  Edit  View  Insert  Format  Tools  Table  Window  Help

Normal        Arial              12      B  I  U

Microsoft Word for Windows

This screen displays what you would see on the computer screen after starting
Microsoft Word for Windows.

Microsoft Word for Windows is one of the most popular Windows-based word
processors.

Page 1   Sec 1    1/1    At 2.1"  Ln 7    Col 12   9:01 AM  REC  MRK  EXT  OVR  WPH
```

INSERTION POINT

The flashing line on a screen is called the insertion point, or cursor. It indicates where the text you type will appear.

WORD WRAPPING

When typing text in a word processor, you do not need to press **Enter** on the keyboard when you reach the end of a line. A word processor automatically moves the text to the next line. This is called word wrapping.

You only need to press **Enter** when you want to start a new line or paragraph.

When you use a word processor to type a letter, the text au...

When you use a word processor to type a letter, the text automatically wraps to the next line as you type.

WORD PROCESSING

EDIT A DOCUMENT

A word processor lets you easily make changes to text in a document.

This sentence moves forward as you type.

⬇

------------------------->This sentence moves forward as you type.

ADD TEXT

You can easily add new text to a document. The existing text automatically moves to make room for the new text.

You can use the delete key to remove text from your document

DELETE TEXT

You can delete text you no longer need. The remaining text automatically moves to fill the empty space.

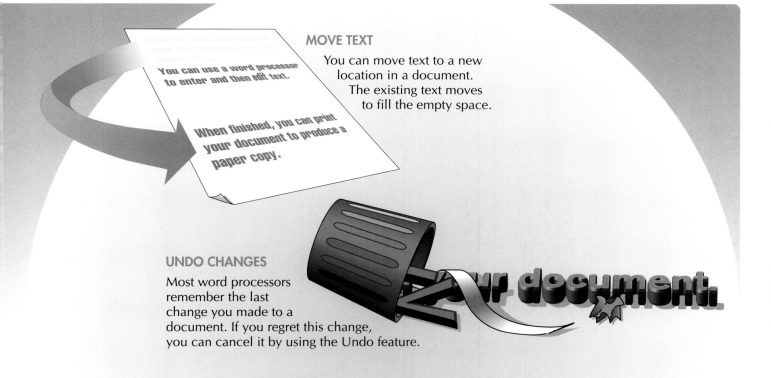

You can use a word processor to enter and then edit text.

When finished, you can print your document to produce a paper copy.

MOVE TEXT

You can move text to a new location in a document. The existing text moves to fill the empty space.

UNDO CHANGES

Most word processors remember the last change you made to a document. If you regret this change, you can cancel it by using the Undo feature.

LONG DOCUMENTS

If you create a long document, your computer screen cannot display all the text at the same time. You must scroll up or down to view and edit other parts of the document.

WORD PROCESSING

SMART EDITING

A word processor provides powerful features to help you edit a document more efficiently.

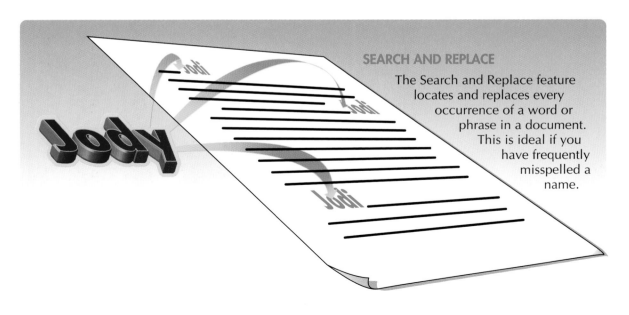

SEARCH AND REPLACE

The Search and Replace feature locates and replaces every occurrence of a word or phrase in a document. This is ideal if you have frequently misspelled a name.

APPLICATION SOFTWARE

- • **Word Processing**
- • Spreadsheets
- • Databases
- • Desktop Publishing
- • Suites

SPELL CHECK

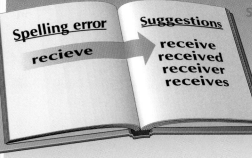

A spell check will find and correct spelling errors in a document. However, it will not find a correctly spelled word used in the wrong context.

Example: The girl is **sit** years old.

Some programs will correct common spelling errors as you type.

Example: **adn** will automatically change to **and**.

THESAURUS

A thesaurus helps you add variety to your writing. This feature lets you replace a word in a document with one that is more suitable.

GRAMMAR CHECK

A grammar check improves the accuracy of a document by looking for grammar, punctuation and stylistic errors.

WORD PROCESSING

A word processor offers many features that let you change the appearance of pages in a document.

COLUMNS

Most word processors can display text in columns like those found in a newspaper. This feature is useful for creating documents such as newsletters and brochures.

MARGINS

A margin is the space between text and an edge of your paper. You can change the margin settings to shorten or lengthen a document or to accommodate letterhead or other specialty paper. Most word processors automatically set a one inch margin on all four sides of a page.

PAGE NUMBERING

A word processor can automatically number the pages in a document. You can specify the position and style of the page numbers.

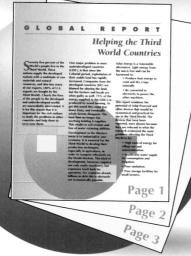

HEADERS AND FOOTERS

You can use headers and footers to print information at the top or bottom of each page in a document. This information may include the title of the document, the date or your company name.

• A **header** appears at the top of a page.

• A **footer** appears at the bottom of a page.

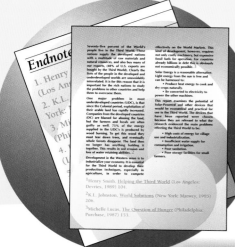

FOOTNOTES AND ENDNOTES

Footnotes and endnotes provide additional information about text in a document.

• A **footnote** appears at the bottom of the page that contains the footnote number.

• **Endnotes** appear at the end of a document.

WORD PROCESSING

PARAGRAPH FORMATTING

When you use a word processor to create a document, you can easily change the appearance of paragraphs.

Goals for the end of the

- Pay off the mor
- Save money fo vacation
- Finish painti house
- Join a healt
- Read more
- Do volun the comm

Recipe

1. Preheat oven to 300°F.
2. Grate 1 cup of cheese.
3. Dice 1/4 cup of onions.
4. Slice 1/2 a red pepper into thin strips.
5. Add cheese, onions and red pepper to meat sauce.
6. Bake for 20 minutes.

BULLETED AND NUMBERED LISTS

You can emphasize text in a list by beginning each item with a bullet or number.

Bullets are useful for items in no particular order, such as a list of goals.

Numbers are useful for items in a specific order, such as a recipe.

TABS

You can use tabs to line up columns of information in a document.

To ensure the document prints correctly, use tabs rather than spaces to line up columns of text.

Last Name	First Name	Address	City	State	Zip Code
Appleton	Jill	456 John Street	Portland	OR	97526
DeVries	Monica	12 Willow Avenue	Los Angeles	CA	90032
Grossi	Rob	23 Riverbead Road	Seattle	WA	98109
Knill	Mark	97 Speers Road	Denver	CO	80207
Leung	Justin	15 Lakeshore Drive	Atlanta	GA	30367
Matwey	Jennifer	34 Kerr Street	Provo	UT	84604
S		56 Devon Road	Dallas	TX	75236

In this example, spaces were used to line up the columns.

Last Name	First Name	Address	City	State	Zip Code
Appleton	Jill	456 John Street	Portland	OR	97526
DeVries	Monica	12 Willow Avenue	Los Angeles	CA	90032
Grossi	Rob	23 Riverbead Road	Seattle	WA	98109
Knill	Mark	97 Speers Road	Denver	CO	80207
Leung	Justin	15 Lakeshore Drive	Atlanta	GA	30367
Matwey	Jennifer	34 Kerr Street	Provo	UT	84604
Smith	Albert	56 Devon Road	Dallas	TX	75236
Smith	Betty	111 Linton Street	Los Angeles	CA	90071
Smith	Carol	36 Ford Drive	Santa Clara	CA	95054
Anderson	David	55 Kennedy Road	Buffalo	NY	14213

In this example, tabs were used to line up the columns.

APPLICATION SOFTWARE

- • **Word Processing**
- • Spreadsheets
- • Databases
- • Desktop Publishing
- • Suites

JUSTIFY TEXT

You can enhance the appearance of a document by aligning text in different ways.

Right

Center

Left

Full

INDENT TEXT

You can emphasize a paragraph in a document by indenting the text. This moves the text farther away from the left or right side of the page.

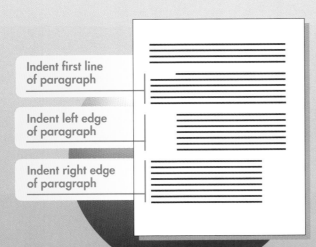

Indent first line of paragraph

Indent left edge of paragraph

Indent right edge of paragraph

LINE SPACING

You can make a document easier to read by changing the amount of space between the lines of text.

Single spacing

1.5 spacing

Double spacing

WORD PROCESSING

You can change the appearance of characters in a document. This lets you emphasize headings and make the document more appealing.

CHARACTER FORMATTING

You can change the font of text in a document.
A font consists of three elements.

TYPEFACE

Typeface refers to the design of characters. Some examples are:

Avante Garde

Bodoni

Courier

Helvetica

Optima

Times New Roman

TYPE SIZE

Type size refers to the size of characters and is measured in points. Most business documents use 10 or 12 point type.

Note: There are approximately 72 points in one inch.

5 point
10 point
15 point
20 point
25 point

TYPE STYLE

Type style refers to the appearance of characters. Some examples are:

Bold

Italic

<u>Underline</u>

Shadow

Outline

~~Strikeout~~

Text^Superscript

Text~Subscript

- **Word Processing**
- Spreadsheets
- Databases
- Desktop Publishing
- Suites

SPECIAL FEATURES

A word processor offers special features that will save you time and make your document more interesting.

TABLES

Word processors let you create a table to organize your information. You can later add colors and borders to enhance the appearance of the table.

MAIL MERGE

Word processors offer a merge feature that lets you produce personalized letters and envelopes for each person on a mailing list.

GRAPHICS

Graphics are pictures that you can add to a document to make it more attractive and interesting. Most word processors offer a few graphics. You can also create or buy additional graphics (example: clip art).

SPREADSHEETS

A spreadsheet program helps you manage, analyze and present information.

HOW YOU CAN USE A SPREADSHEET

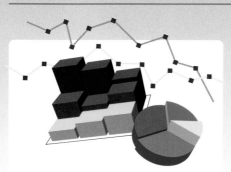

CHARTS

You can create charts from spreadsheet data. Charts illustrate the relationship between different items.

PERSONAL FINANCES

A spreadsheet can help you keep track of your personal finances. You can use a spreadsheet to:

- balance your checkbook
- create a budget
- keep track of your mortgage
- compare investments
- prepare your taxes

FINANCIAL REPORTS

Businesses of all sizes use spreadsheets to analyze and present financial information. Formatting and charting features help you present your results in professional-looking documents.

SPREADSHEET BASICS

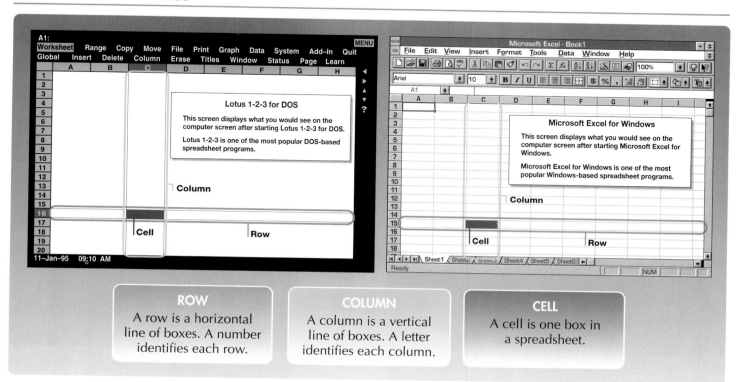

Lotus 1-2-3 for DOS

This screen displays what you would see on the computer screen after starting Lotus 1-2-3 for DOS.

Lotus 1-2-3 is one of the most popular DOS-based spreadsheet programs.

Microsoft Excel for Windows

This screen displays what you would see on the computer screen after starting Microsoft Excel for Windows.

Microsoft Excel for Windows is one of the most popular Windows-based spreadsheet programs.

ROW
A row is a horizontal line of boxes. A number identifies each row.

COLUMN
A column is a vertical line of boxes. A letter identifies each column.

CELL
A cell is one box in a spreadsheet.

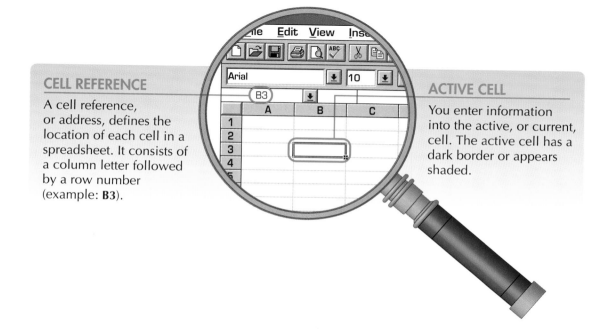

CELL REFERENCE
A cell reference, or address, defines the location of each cell in a spreadsheet. It consists of a column letter followed by a row number (example: **B3**).

ACTIVE CELL
You enter information into the active, or current, cell. The active cell has a dark border or appears shaded.

163

SPREADSHEETS

You can use formulas to perform calculations on data in a spreadsheet. For example, you can use a formula to add a list of numbers.

FORMULAS

You can use these operators in a formula:

+	Addition
-	Subtraction
*	Multiplication
/	Division
^	Exponentiation

When entering formulas, use cell references (example: A1) instead of actual numbers whenever possible. This way, if data changes, the program will automatically redo the calculations for you.

	A	B	C	D	E	F
1	10		10		10	
2	20		20		20	
3	30		30		30	
4	40		40		40	
5						
6	100		210		72	
7						

Cell A6 contains the formula:

=A1+A2+A3+A4

=10+20+30+40

=100

Cell C6 contains the formula:

=C1*C2-C3+C4

=10*20-30+40

=210

Cell E6 contains the formula:

=E2/E1+E3+E4

=20/10+30+40

=72

- Word Processing
- **Spreadsheets**
- Databases
- Desktop Publishing
- Suites

> Spreadsheet programs offer ready-to-use formulas, called functions. Functions let you perform calculations without typing long, complex formulas.

FUNCTIONS

MAX SUM AVERAGE

	A	B	C	D	E	F
1	10		10		10	
2	20		20		20	
3	30		30		30	
4	60		60		60	
5						
6	120		30		60	
7						

The SUM function adds a list of numbers.

Cell A6 contains the function:

=SUM(A1:A4)

=A1+A2+A3+A4

=10+20+30+60

=120

The AVERAGE function calculates the average value of a list of numbers.

Cell C6 contains the function:

=AVERAGE(C1:C4)

=(C1+C2+C3+C4)/4

=(10+20+30+60)/4

=30

The MAX function finds the largest value in a list of numbers.

Cell E6 contains the function:

=MAX(E1:E4)

=60

SPREADSHEETS

If you change a number in a spreadsheet, you do not have to manually redo all the calculations. The spreadsheet will automatically recalculate the results for you.

WHAT-IF ANALYSIS

When you change data in a spreadsheet, you can see the effects on the rest of the data. This is useful for evaluating several possible scenarios.

For example, if interest rates go down, how will this affect my car and mortgage payments? If the cost of goods decreases by 10%, how will this affect my profits?

AUTOMATIC RECALCULATION

	Jan	Feb	Total
Unit 1	100	120	220
Unit 2	300	340	640
Total	400	460	860

400

◆ In this example, the number 340 is changed to 400.

	Jan	Feb	Total
Unit 1	100	120	220
Unit 2	300	400	700
Total	400	520	920

◆ The spreadsheet recalculates all the formulas using the new number.

APPLICATION SOFTWARE

- Word Processing
- **Spreadsheets**
- Databases
- Desktop Publishing
- Suites

Spreadsheet programs provide many features to enhance the appearance of data.

FORMAT A SPREADSHEET

1037.82

Scientific	1.04E+03
Currency	$1,037.82
Comma	1,037.82
General	1037.82
Percent	103782%

FORMAT NUMBERS

You can change the appearance of numbers in a spreadsheet without retyping them. This can make the numbers easier to understand.

INCOME STATEMENT

INCOME STATEMENT

INCOME STATEMENT

INCOME STATEMENT

INCOME STATEMENT

	Jan	Feb	Mar	Total
REVENUE	$10,500	$11,500	$13,670	$35,670
Payroll	$3,850	$4,850	$5,250	$13,950
Rent	$1,750	$1,750	$1,750	$5,250
Supplies	$1,920	$1,980	$2,030	$5,930
TOTAL EXPENSES	$7,520	$8,580	$9,030	$25,130
INCOME	$2,980	$2,920	$4,640	$10,540

USING FONTS

You can change the design and size of characters in a spreadsheet to emphasize headings and make data easier to read.

Note: For more information on fonts, refer to page 160.

ADD LINES, SHADING AND COLOR

You can add lines, shading and color to draw attention to data and improve the appearance of a spreadsheet. Some programs provide a selection of designs that you can use to quickly format a spreadsheet.

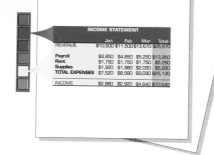

SPREADSHEETS

Spreadsheet programs let you visually display data in a chart.

CHARTS

You can create a chart directly from data in a spreadsheet.

	Jan	Feb	Total
Unit 1	100	120	220
Unit 2	300	340	640
Total	400	460	860

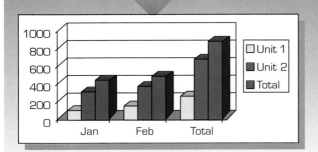

CHART TYPES

Spreadsheet programs offer many types of charts. These range from simple line charts to three-dimensional charts. After creating a chart, you can select a new type that will better suit the data.

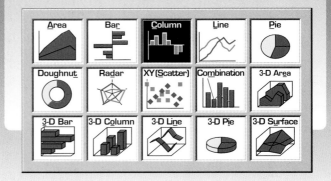

APPLICATION SOFTWARE

- Word Processing
- Spreadsheets
- Databases
- Desktop Publishing
- Suites

SPECIAL FEATURES

Spreadsheets offer special features to help you efficiently enter, manage and present information.

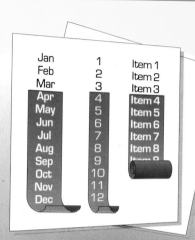

COMPLETE A SERIES

Many spreadsheet programs can save you time by completing a series of labels or numbers for you.

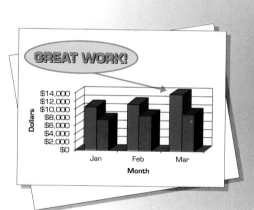

DRAW OBJECTS

Many spreadsheet programs let you draw shapes and lines to emphasize specific areas of a spreadsheet.

MANAGE DATA IN A LIST

Most spreadsheet programs provide tools for managing a list of information. You can quickly find specific information in a list or change the order of the information.

A database program acts as your own personal assistant. It organizes, sorts, retrieves and compares information for you.

A database program helps you manage large collections of information.

PAYROLL 1995

PAYROLL 1990

Common databases include mailing lists, library book catalogs, product listings and payrolls.

DATABASE APPLICATIONS

STORE DATA

You can use a database to keep large collections of information organized and up-to-date.

ANALYZE DATA

You can use the information stored in a database to help you make quick, accurate and informed decisions. For example, you can decide which product line to expand due to increasing profits.

CREATE LABELS, LETTERS AND ENVELOPES

You can use the information stored in a database to quickly create letters, envelopes and labels for large mailings. You can target specific groups in your database, such as customers who have spent over $100 in the past month.

CREATE REPORTS

You can perform calculations, such as totals or averages, on the information in a database. You can then examine the results to develop marketing strategies or create reports and presentations.

DATABASE TERMS

A table is a collection of data about a particular subject, such as the addresses of all employees.

EMPLOYEE INFORMATION

Last Name	First Name	Street	City	State	Zip Code
Smith	John	258 Linton Ave.	New York	NY	10010
Lang	Kristin	50 Tree Lane	Boston	MA	02117
Oram	Derek	68 Cacker Ave.	San Francisco	CA	94110
Gray	Russel	1 Hollywood Blvd.	Cincinnati	OH	45217
Atherley	Peter	47 Cosby Ave.	Las Vegas	NV	89116
Talbot	Mark	26 Arnold Cres.	Jacksonville	FL	32256
Coleman	Duane	401 Idon Dr.	Nashville	TN	37243
Sanvido	Dean	16 Hoover Cres.	Greenwich	CT	06831
Slater	Mark	468 Starewell Rd.	Salem	MA	97304
Pozeg	Dan	10 Heldon St.	Atlanta	GA	30367
Hretchka	Steve	890 Apple St.	San Diego	CA	92121
Gombocz	Sandor	18 Goulage Ave.	Los Angeles	CA	90032
Boshart	Mark	36 Buzzard St.	Denver	CO	
Jaklitsch	Janet	15 Bizzo Pl.	Portland	OR	
Lippert	Diane				
Allison					

◆ **FIELD NAME**
Each field has a name to distinguish it from other fields. Field names help to ensure that you enter the correct data in the proper locations.

◆ **RECORD**
A record is a collection of data about one person, place or thing.

◆ **FIELD**
A field is a category of data, such as the first names of all employees.

PRODUCT INFORMATION

Product Number	Employee ID	Phone Number
CT89238	39650	(905)-555-2952
LN29295	20639	(905)-555-2856
PT39206	30924	(905)-555-2597
JS22948	29505	(905)-555-2058
MN25694	43247	(905)-55...
T43776		

◆ To prevent errors when entering data, you can restrict each field to accept only a certain number of characters. For example, you can only enter seven characters into this field.

◆ You can restrict each field to accept only a certain type of data. For example, you can only enter numbers (0 to 9) into this field. Letters (A to Z) are not allowed.

◆ To make data easier to enter and read, you can have a database program format data for you. For example, if you enter 1234567890 into this field, the program will change the number to (123)-456-7890.

LOCATING INFORMATION IN A DATABASE

SORT DATA

You can change the order of information in a database. For example, you can alphabetically sort all employees by last name.

BROWSE

You can browse through the information in a database. This is similar to scanning a newspaper for interesting articles.

FIND DATA

You can quickly find information stored in a database. A **query** is a question you ask to find the information you need. For example, you can search for employees who sold more than 1000 units last month.

173

DATABASES

A relational database contains two or more tables that share common information.

RELATIONAL DATABASE

Relational databases are powerful and flexible, but complicated to set up and learn. They are often used for accounting purposes.

Relational databases let you combine data from different tables to create invoices or reports. For example, you can combine order and product information to quickly create an invoice.

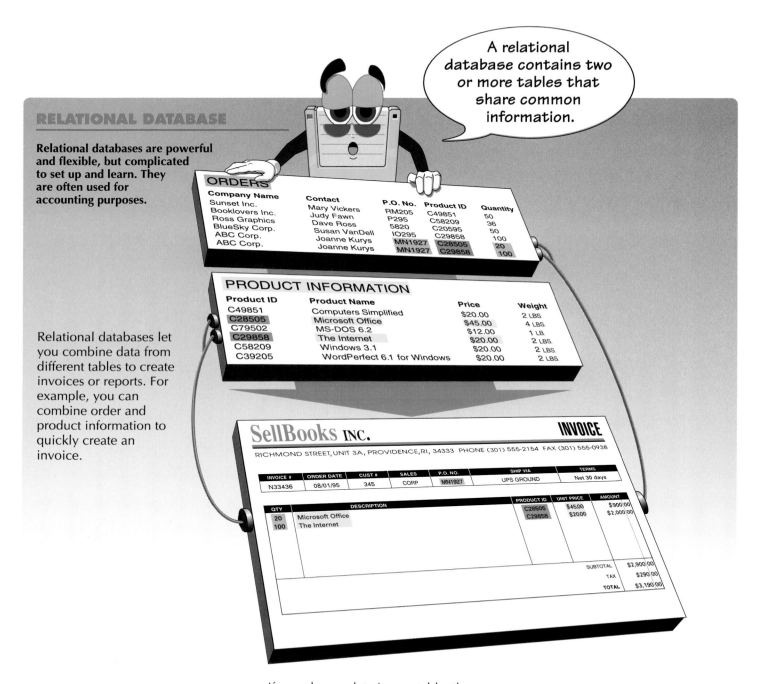

If you change data in one table, the data will change in all related tables. This saves you time because you only have to change the data once.

- Word Processing
- Spreadsheets
- Databases
- Desktop Publishing
- Suites

FLAT FILE DATABASE

A flat file database is a single table that does not share information with other tables.

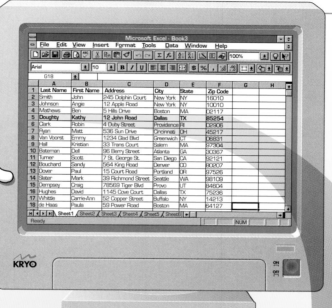

Kathy Doughty
12 John Road
Dallas, TX
85254

This type of database is ideal for single-purpose use, such as an address book or client phone number list.

Flat file databases are easy to set up and learn.

Tip Popular database programs include Access, dBASE and FoxPro.

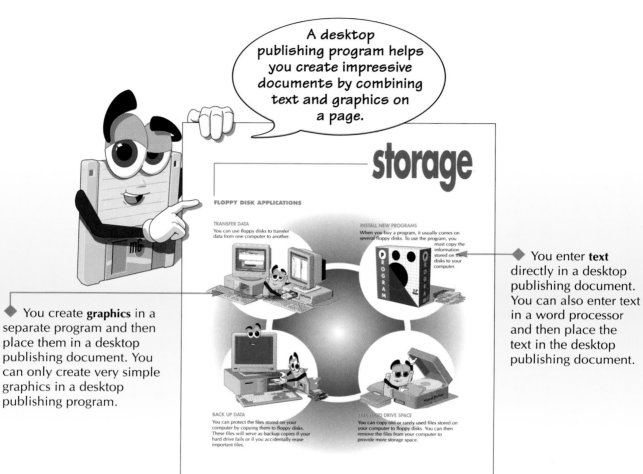

A desktop publishing program helps you create impressive documents by combining text and graphics on a page.

You create **graphics** in a separate program and then place them in a desktop publishing document. You can only create very simple graphics in a desktop publishing program.

You enter **text** directly in a desktop publishing document. You can also enter text in a word processor and then place the text in the desktop publishing document.

You can use a desktop publishing program to create newsletters, brochures, manuals, books, flyers, advertisements and magazines.

Popular desktop publishing programs include Adobe PageMaker, Corel Publisher, Microsoft Publisher and QuarkXPress.

APPLICATION SOFTWARE

- Word Processing
- Spreadsheets
- Databases
- **Desktop Publishing**
- Suites

GRAPHICS

These are some of the changes you can make to graphics in a desktop publishing program.

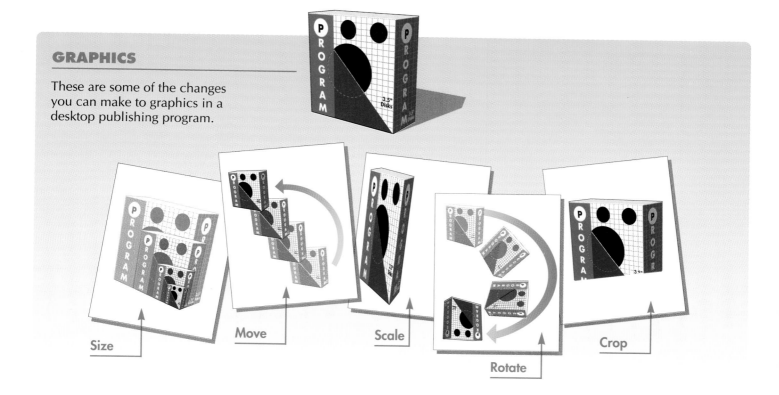

Size

Move

Scale

Rotate

Crop

TEXT

These are some of the changes you can make to text in a desktop publishing program.

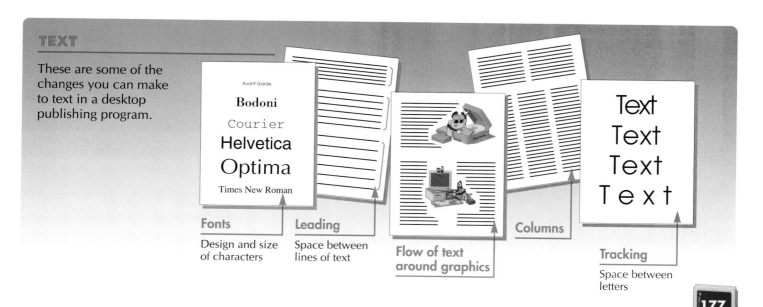

Avant Garde

Bodoni

Courier

Helvetica

Optima

Times New Roman

Fonts
Design and size of characters

Leading
Space between lines of text

Flow of text around graphics

Columns

Tracking
Space between letters

SUITES

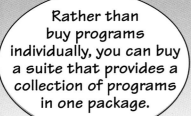

Rather than buy programs individually, you can buy a suite that provides a collection of programs in one package.

ADVANTAGES

- It costs less to buy programs as part of a suite than to buy them individually.

- Programs look and act the same. Once you learn one program, you can easily learn the others.

- Programs can exchange data and interact in ways they cannot do alone.

DISADVANTAGE

- When you buy programs in a suite, you are buying programs from one manufacturer. You may not get the best combination of programs for your specific needs.

MICROSOFT OFFICE

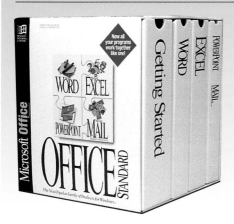

WORD
A word processing program that lets you create documents such as letters, reports and newsletters.

EXCEL
A spreadsheet program that lets you manage and analyze information.

POWERPOINT
A presentation program that lets you plan, organize and design presentations.

MAIL
An electronic mail program that lets you exchange messages with other people on a network.

The Professional version of Microsoft Office includes all of these programs, plus Access.

Access is a database program that lets you manage large collections of information.

- Word Processing
- Spreadsheets
- Databases
- Desktop Publishing
- **Suites**

LOTUS SMARTSUITE

AMI PRO
A word processing program that lets you create documents such as letters, reports and newsletters.

1-2-3
A spreadsheet program that lets you manage and analyze information.

FREELANCE GRAPHICS
A presentation program that lets you plan, organize and design presentations.

ORGANIZER
A personal information manager that lets you keep track of appointments and other events.

APPROACH
A database program that lets you manage large collections of information.

NOVELL PERFECTOFFICE

WORDPERFECT
A word processing program that lets you create documents such as letters, reports and newsletters.

QUATTRO PRO
A spreadsheet program that lets you manage and analyze information.

PRESENTATIONS
A presentation program that lets you plan, organize and design presentations.

INFOCENTRAL
A personal information manager that lets you keep track of appointments and other events.

GROUPWISE
An office manager that includes electronic mail, scheduling and task management features.

ENVOY
A program that lets other people view a document, even if their computers do not have the program that created the document.

The Professional version of PerfectOffice includes all of these programs, plus Paradox and Visual AppBuilder.

Paradox is a database program that lets you manage large collections of information. Visual AppBuilder is a programming tool that lets you develop applications using visual techniques rather than programming code.

179

NETWORKS

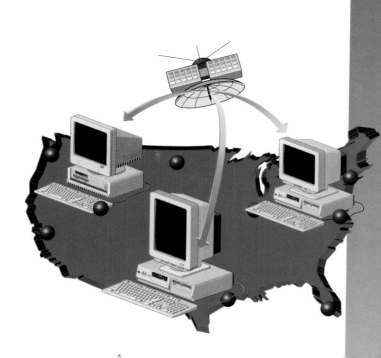

INTRODUCTION TO NETWORKS

NETWORK ADVANTAGES

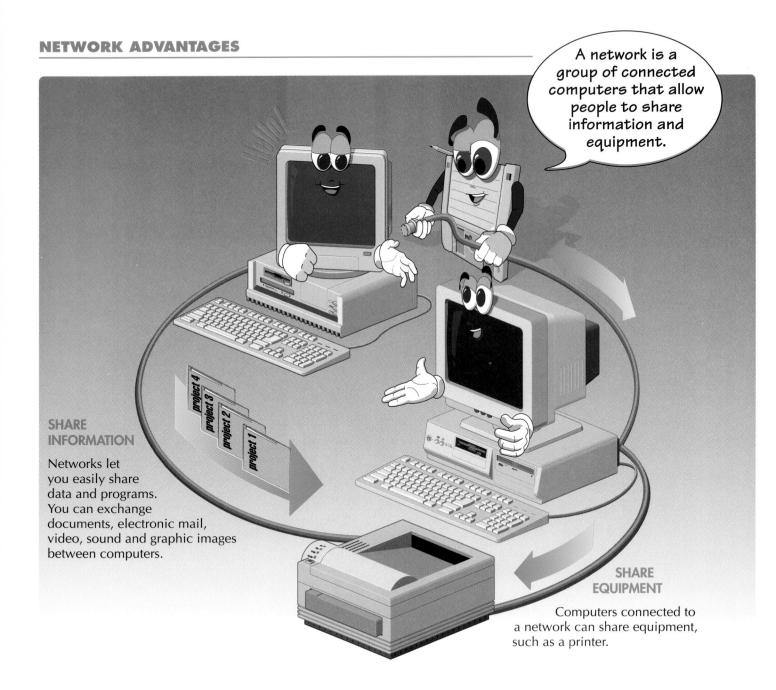

A network is a group of connected computers that allow people to share information and equipment.

SHARE INFORMATION

Networks let you easily share data and programs. You can exchange documents, electronic mail, video, sound and graphic images between computers.

SHARE EQUIPMENT

Computers connected to a network can share equipment, such as a printer.

NETWORKS

- **Introduction to Networks**
- Common Network Terms
- Network Applications
- Network Security
- Peer-to-Peer Network
- Client/Server Network
- Ethernet
- Token-Ring
- On-line Services

LOCAL AND WIDE AREA NETWORKS

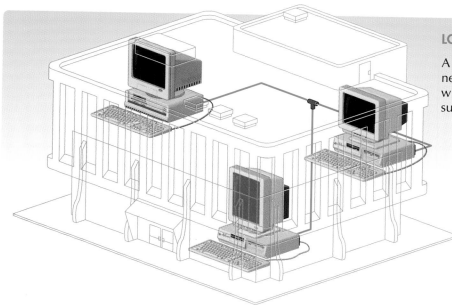

LOCAL AREA NETWORK

A Local Area Network (LAN) is a network that connects computers within a small geographic area, such as an office or building.

WIDE AREA NETWORK

A Wide Area Network (WAN) is a network that connects computers across a large geographic area, such as a city or country. A WAN can transmit information by telephone line, microwave or satellite.

The Internet is a WAN that connects millions of people around the world.

Note: For more information on the Internet, refer to page 193.

183

COMMON NETWORK TERMS

WORKSTATION

A workstation, or node, is a single computer connected to a network.

PERIPHERAL

A peripheral is a device connected to a network that all computers on the network can use. Peripherals include printers, modems and scanners.

NETWORK OPERATING SYSTEM

A network operating system is a program that manages the sharing of information and peripherals on a network. This program acts like a traffic cop, controlling the flow of information through a network.

NETWORK TRAFFIC

Network traffic is the information sent through a network. This can include anything from a word processing document to a graphic image.

- Introduction to Networks
- **Common Network Terms**
- Network Applications
- Network Security
- Peer-to-Peer Network
- Client/Server Network
- Ethernet
- Token-Ring
- On-line Services

CABLES

Cables connect computers and peripherals to a network.

MODEM

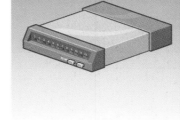

A modem is a device that allows computers to communicate through telephone lines. This lets computers in different buildings exchange information.

NETWORK ADMINISTRATOR

A network administrator manages the network and makes sure it runs smoothly.

NETWORK INTERFACE CARD

A network interface card physically connects each computer to the network. This card packages the data you want to send and controls the flow of information to and from the network.

NETWORK APPLICATIONS

GROUPWARE

Groupware is software that improves the productivity of people working on a related project.

Groupware lets several people work with the same file at once. It also helps people coordinate and manage activities. For example, you can check the schedule of each person on a network to decide what time is best to have a meeting.

ELECTRONIC MAIL

Electronic mail (e-mail) lets you exchange messages with other people on a network. This saves paper and provides a fast and convenient way of scheduling appointments, exchanging ideas and requesting information. Most e-mail programs let you send the same message to more than one person at a time.

NETWORK SECURITY

A network should have security measures to protect files from damage or misuse.

You can purchase programs that detect and eliminate viruses.

VIRUSES

A virus is a program that can multiply and spread through a network. Some viruses destroy or alter data, while others attempt to shut down the network.

PASSWORDS

You usually have to enter a password to gain access to a network. This ensures that only authorized personnel can use the files stored on the network.

Follow these guidelines when creating a password:

- The most effective password connects two words or number sequences with a special character (example: easy@123).

- Never write down your password.

- Change your password every few weeks.

- Do not use words that people can easily associate with you, such as your name or favorite sport.

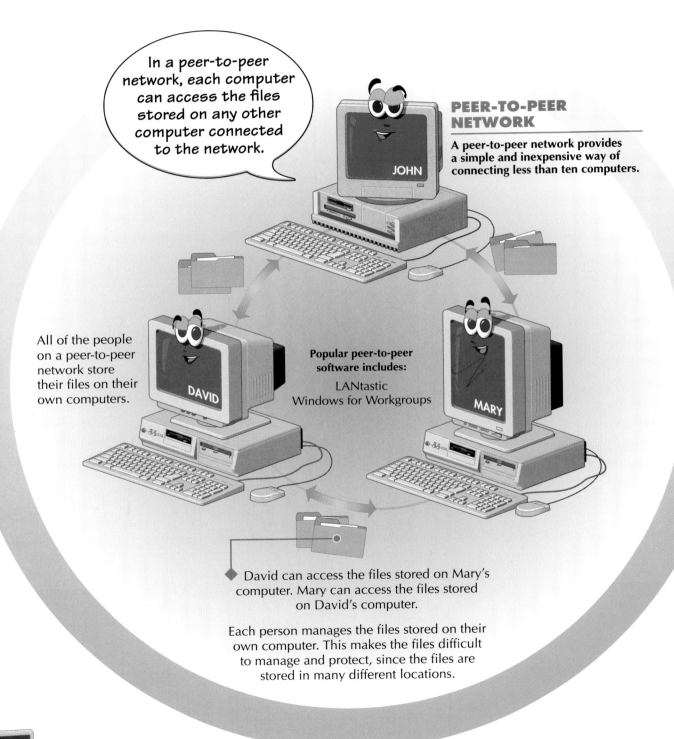

In a peer-to-peer network, each computer can access the files stored on any other computer connected to the network.

PEER-TO-PEER NETWORK

A peer-to-peer network provides a simple and inexpensive way of connecting less than ten computers.

All of the people on a peer-to-peer network store their files on their own computers.

Popular peer-to-peer software includes:

LANtastic
Windows for Workgroups

◆ David can access the files stored on Mary's computer. Mary can access the files stored on David's computer.

Each person manages the files stored on their own computer. This makes the files difficult to manage and protect, since the files are stored in many different locations.

> In a client/server network, each person stores their files on the server. Everyone connected to the network can access these files.

CLIENT/SERVER NETWORK

A client/server network provides a highly efficient way of connecting computers to share information. **Companies with ten or more computers and those exchanging large amounts of data use a client/server network.**

A **server** is a computer that stores the files of every person connected to the network. Since all the files are stored in a central location, they are easy to manage and protect.

Popular client/server software includes:

VINES
LAN Manager
NetWare
Windows NT

David and Mary store their files on the server. This lets each person connected to the network access the files.

David and Mary are clients. A **client** is a computer that can access information stored on a server.

189

ETHERNET

Ethernet works the same way people talk during a polite conversation. Each computer waits for a pause before sending information through the network.

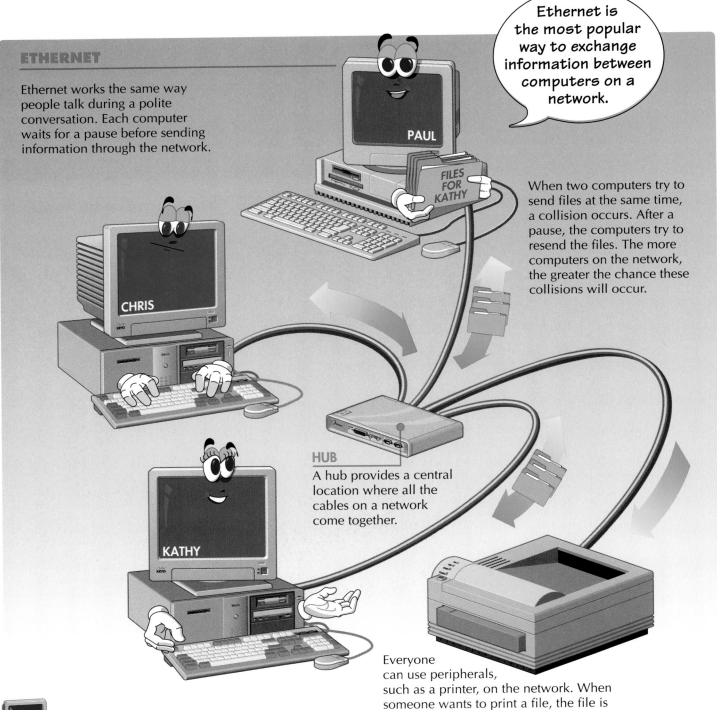

Ethernet is the most popular way to exchange information between computers on a network.

When two computers try to send files at the same time, a collision occurs. After a pause, the computers try to resend the files. The more computers on the network, the greater the chance these collisions will occur.

HUB
A hub provides a central location where all the cables on a network come together.

Everyone can use peripherals, such as a printer, on the network. When someone wants to print a file, the file is sent across the network to the printer.

TOKEN-RING

Token-ring works by passing a single token from computer to computer around the network. To send a file, a computer must wait for the token to reach it, attach the file to the token and then return both the token and the file to the network.

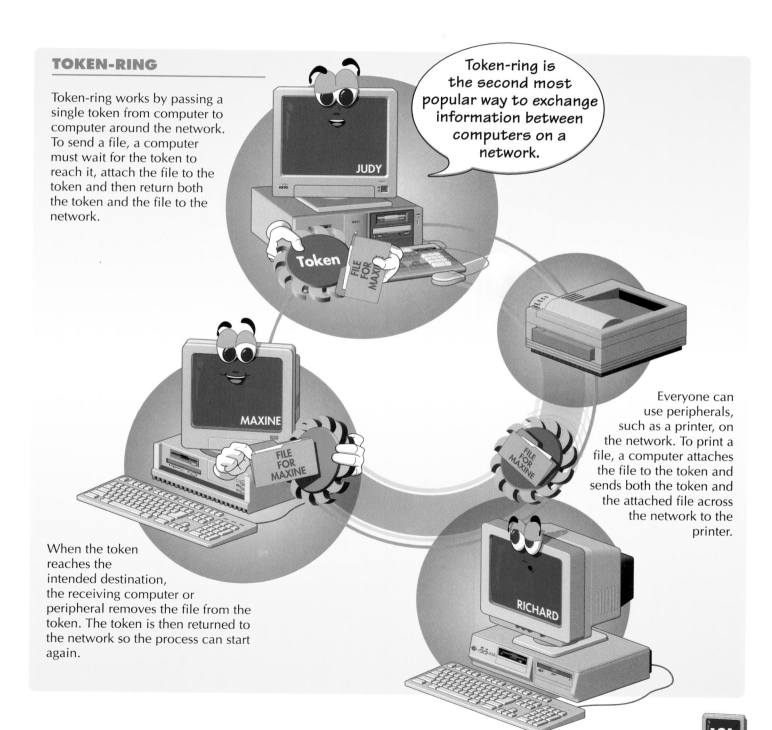

Token-ring is the second most popular way to exchange information between computers on a network.

Everyone can use peripherals, such as a printer, on the network. To print a file, a computer attaches the file to the token and sends both the token and the attached file across the network to the printer.

When the token reaches the intended destination, the receiving computer or peripheral removes the file from the token. The token is then returned to the network so the process can start again.

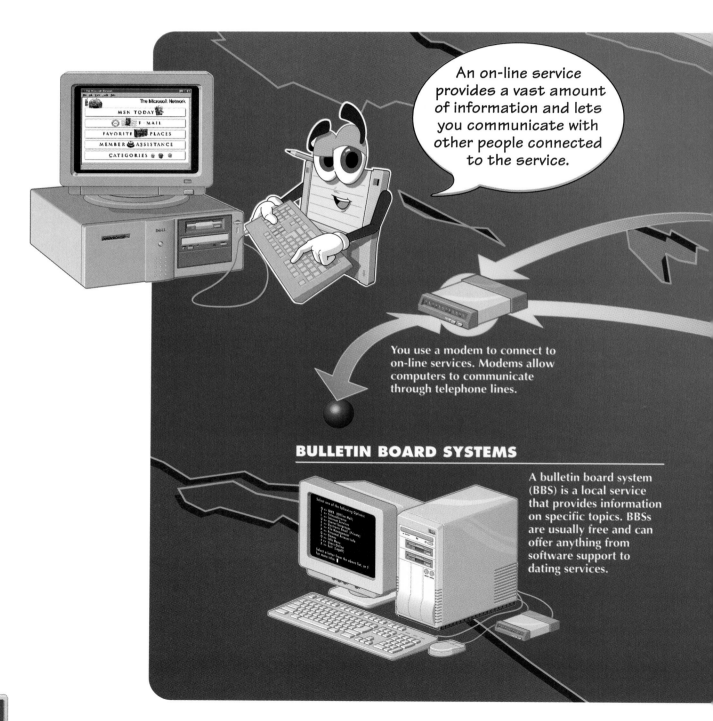

An on-line service provides a vast amount of information and lets you communicate with other people connected to the service.

You use a modem to connect to on-line services. Modems allow computers to communicate through telephone lines.

BULLETIN BOARD SYSTEMS

A bulletin board system (BBS) is a local service that provides information on specific topics. BBSs are usually free and can offer anything from software support to dating services.

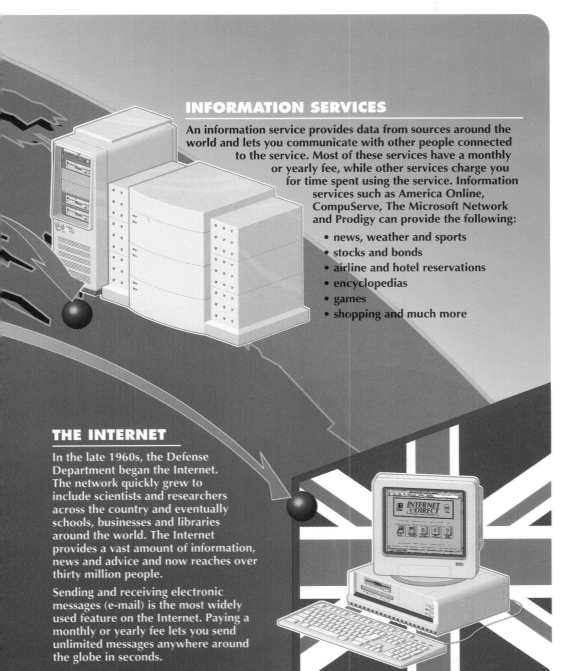

INFORMATION SERVICES

An information service provides data from sources around the world and lets you communicate with other people connected to the service. Most of these services have a monthly or yearly fee, while other services charge you for time spent using the service. Information services such as America Online, CompuServe, The Microsoft Network and Prodigy can provide the following:

- news, weather and sports
- stocks and bonds
- airline and hotel reservations
- encyclopedias
- games
- shopping and much more

THE INTERNET

In the late 1960s, the Defense Department began the Internet. The network quickly grew to include scientists and researchers across the country and eventually schools, businesses and libraries around the world. The Internet provides a vast amount of information, news and advice and now reaches over thirty million people.

Sending and receiving electronic messages (e-mail) is the most widely used feature on the Internet. Paying a monthly or yearly fee lets you send unlimited messages anywhere around the globe in seconds.

GLOSSARY

386
A type of CPU found in old computers. It is now obsolete.

486
A type of CPU that processes one instruction at a time.

486DX
A type of CPU that includes a built-in math coprocessor to perform complex math calculations.

486DX2
A type of CPU that is twice as fast as a 486DX chip.

486DX4
A type of CPU that is three times as fast as a 486DX chip.

486SX
A type of CPU that does not include a built-in math coprocessor.

A

Access Time
The amount of time it takes a device to retrieve information.

Active Cell
The cell in a spreadsheet where you enter data. It has a dark border or appears shaded. Also called the current cell.

Active Matrix Screen
A type of screen used in portable computers that displays bright, rich colors. It is easy to view from an angle, which makes it ideal for delivering presentations to several people.

Anti-Glare Screen
A transparent screen that fits over the front of a monitor. It decreases the amount of light reflected off the computer screen to reduce eye strain.

B

Backlighting
An internal light source at the back of a portable. It makes the screen easier to view in low-light areas.

Backup
A copy of data to be used in case the original data is damaged or destroyed.

Battery
A device that powers a portable computer when no electrical outlets are available.

Buffer
A section of memory in a printer that stores information you selected to print.

Bulletin Board System (BBS)
A local network service that provides information on specific topics.

Bus
The electronic pathway in a computer that carries information between devices.

Byte
One character. It can be a number, letter or symbol.

C

Carpal Tunnel Syndrome
A condition of numbness, tingling and pain in the fingers. It affects workers who type without proper wrist support or type for long periods of time without breaks.

Case
A device that contains all the major components of a computer system.

CD-ROM Drive
Compact Disc-Read Only Memory drive. A device that reads information stored on compact discs.

Cell
A single box in a spreadsheet or table.

Cell Reference
Defines the location of each cell in a spreadsheet or table. It consists of a column letter followed by a row number (example: A2). Also called a cell address.

Chart
Illustrates the relationship between items. Also called a graph.

Client
A computer on a network that can access information stored on a server.

Client/Server Network
A type of network where each person stores their files on a server. All computers connected to the network can access the files.

Column
A vertical line of boxes in a spreadsheet or table.

Command
An instruction that tells a computer to perform a specific task.

Compression
The process of squeezing together information so it takes up less room.

CPU
Central Processing Unit. The main chip that processes instructions, performs calculations and manages the flow of information through a computer system. Also called a microprocessor.

Cursor
A flashing line on a computer screen. It indicates where information you enter will appear. Also called an insertion point.

D

Database
A program that helps you manage large collections of information.

DAT Drive
Digital Audio Tape drive. A type of tape drive that is ideal for backing up information stored on a network.

Defragmentation
The process of placing all parts of each file on a hard drive in one location to improve performance.

GLOSSARY

Desktop Case
A flat, wide computer case that usually sits on a desk, under a monitor.

Desktop Publishing
A program that helps you create impressive documents by combining text and graphics.

Dialog Box
A small, on-screen window that lets you select options for a specific task.

Directory
Like a folder in a filing cabinet, a directory organizes information stored on a computer.

Disk Cache
Part of a computer's main memory. It stores data recently used by a computer to improve its performance.

Diskette
See Floppy Disk.

Docking Station
A device that lets you quickly connect a portable to multiple devices and extend the capabilities of a portable.

DOS
See MS-DOS.

Dot-Matrix Printer
The least expensive type of printer. It is ideal for printing on multipart forms, which need an impact to print through multiple copies.

Dot Pitch
Measures the clarity of a monitor. The smaller the dot pitch, the crisper the images on the screen.

DRAM
Dynamic Random Access Memory. The most common type of computer memory.

Dye Sublimation Color Printer
A type of printer that produces images that look like color photographs. Also called a thermal dye transfer printer.

E

EIDE
Enhanced Integrated Drive Electronics. A way of connecting hard drives and other devices to a computer.

E-Mail
Messages sent from one person to another through a network.

Endnote
A note providing additional information about text in a document. It appears at the end of a document.

Energy Star
An energy-saving guideline developed by the Environmental Protection Agency. An Energy Star computer enters an energy-saving sleep mode when it is not used for a period of time.

Ergonomics
The science of designing equipment for a comfortable and safe working environment.

Ethernet
A way of exchanging information between computers on a network. It works like a polite conversation. Each computer waits for a pause before sending information through the network.

Expansion Card
A circuit board that adds a new feature, such as CD-quality sound, to a computer.

Expansion Slot
A socket inside a computer where you plug in an expansion card.

F

Field
A category of data in a database, such as the last names of all employees.

Flatbed Scanner
A type of scanner that works like a photocopier to import text and graphics into a computer.

Flat File Database
A type of database that is ideal for single-purpose use, such as an address book.

Floppy Disk
A removable device that magnetically stores data. Also called a diskette.

Floppy Drive
A device that stores and retrieves information on floppy disks.

FM Synthesis
One way that a sound card can produce sound. It creates unrealistic, tinny sound by imitating the sounds of musical instruments.

Font
A set of characters of a particular design and size.

Footer
Information that appears at the bottom of each page in a document.

Footnote
A note providing additional information about text in a document. It appears at the bottom of the page containing the footnote number.

Format
The process of preparing a floppy or hard disk to store information.

Formula
A mathematical statement that performs a calculation.

Fragmentation
A condition found on hard drives when parts of files are stored in many different locations. This slows down a computer.

Function
A ready-to-use formula that performs a calculation.

G

Gigabyte (GB)
Approximately one billion characters.

Groupware
A type of software that improves the productivity of people working on a related project.

GLOSSARY

H

Hand-Held Scanner
A type of scanner that is ideal for importing small images, such as a logo, into a computer.

Handshake
Signals transmitted between modems to establish how the modems will exchange information.

Hard Drive
The primary device that a computer uses to store information.

Hardware
Any part of a computer system that you can see or touch.

Header
Information that appears at the top of each page in a document.

I

Icon
A small picture on a screen that represents an object, such as a file or program.

IDE
Integrated Drive Electronics. An inexpensive way of connecting one or two hard drives to a computer.

Information Service
A dial-up service that provides a vast amount of information and lets you communicate with other people connected to the service. Examples include CompuServe and Prodigy.

Ink Jet Printer
A relatively inexpensive type of printer that is ideal for producing routine office documents.

Insertion Point
See Cursor.

Internet
The world's largest computer network, used by over thirty million people. It provides a vast amount of information, news and advice and lets you communicate with people around the world in seconds.

ISA Bus
Industry Standard Architecture bus. The oldest, slowest and least expensive type of bus.

K

Keyboard
A device connected to a computer and used to enter information and instructions. It includes standard typewriter keys and specialized keys.

Kilobyte (K)
Approximately one thousand characters.

L

Laptop
A type of portable computer that weighs between eight and ten pounds. It is now obsolete.

Laser Printer
A fast, high-quality printer that is ideal for producing routine business and personal documents.

LCD
Liquid Crystal Display. A type of screen used in portable computers and digital wristwatches.

Local Area Network (LAN)

A type of network that connects computers within a small geographic area, such as an office or building.

M

Margin

The space between text and an edge of a page.

Megabyte (MB)

Approximately one million characters.

Memory

See Random Access Memory.

Memory Cache

An area where data recently used by a computer is stored to improve performance.

Menu

Provides a list of related commands that let you accomplish tasks.

MIDI

Musical Instrument Digital Interface. A set of rules that allow computers, synthesizers and musical instruments to exchange information. This lets you use a computer to play, record and edit music.

Modem

A device that lets computers exchange information through telephone lines.

Monitor

A device that displays text and graphics generated by a computer.

Motherboard

The main circuit board of a computer. All electrical components plug into the motherboard.

Mouse

A hand-held device used to select and move items on a screen.

Mouse Pointer

A symbol on a screen, usually ↖, that you can move to select items and move the cursor.

MPC

Multimedia Personal Computer. The requirements for a multimedia computer system, as listed by the Multimedia Personal Computer Marketing Council.

MS-DOS

Microsoft Disk Operating System. A program that controls the overall activity of a computer. It uses text commands you enter to perform tasks.

Multimedia

A combination of graphics, text, video, sound, animation and photographs.

Multisync Monitor

A type of monitor that can display images at various resolutions. This allows you to shrink or expand images on a screen.

GLOSSARY

N

Network
A group of computers connected together to share information and equipment.

Non-Interlaced Monitor
A type of monitor that decreases the amount of screen flicker to reduce eye strain.

Notebook
A type of portable computer that weighs between six and eight pounds and is the size of a three-ring binder.

O

OCR Software
Optical Character Recognition software. Allows a computer to read handwritten or printed text and convert it into characters.

Operating System
A program that controls the overall activity of a computer.

OverDrive CPU
A chip that replaces an existing CPU to increase the processing power of a computer.

P

Palmtop
A hand-held portable computer that weighs less than one pound. It is most often used as a daily organizer.

Parallel Port
A type of socket at the back of a computer where you plug in a printer or tape drive. It has 25 holes.

Passive Matrix Screen
A type of screen used in portable computers. It is difficult to read when viewed from an angle, which is ideal when you want to keep your work private.

PC Card
A lightweight, credit card sized device that adds a new feature to a portable computer. Also called a PCMCIA card.

PCI Bus
Peripheral Component Interconnect bus. The most sophisticated type of bus, used primarily in Pentium computers.

PCL
Printer Control Language. A type of language used by laser printers. It is used for routine office tasks.

Peer-to-Peer Network
A type of network that provides a simple and inexpensive way of connecting less than ten computers to exchange information.

Pentium
A type of CPU that processes two instructions at a time.

Peripheral
A piece of hardware attached to a computer, such as a printer or keyboard.

Plug and Play
The ability to add new features to a computer and immediately use them. It eliminates complicated installation procedures.

Port
A socket at the back of a computer where you plug in an external device, such as a printer.

Portable
A small, lightweight computer that you can easily transport.

Port Replicator
A device that has the same ports as those found on the back of a portable computer. It lets you connect several devices to a portable in one step.

PostScript
A type of language used by laser printers. It is popular in the graphic arts industry.

Power Bar
A device that provides additional power outlets.

Power Supply
A device inside a computer that changes normal household electricity into electricity that a computer can use.

Printer
A device that produces a paper copy of information from a computer.

Q

QIC Drive
Quarter-Inch Cartridge drive. A type of tape drive that is ideal for backing up information stored on a single computer.

Query
A question you ask a computer to find the information you need in a database.

R

Random Access Memory (RAM)
Electronic memory that temporarily stores information inside a computer. This information disappears when you turn off the computer.

Record
A collection of data in a database about a person, place or thing.

Relational Database
A type of database that is powerful and flexible. It is often used for accounting purposes.

Resolution
The amount of detail or sharpness of an image.

Row
A horizontal line of boxes in a spreadsheet or table.

S

Scanner
A device that translates information it sees on a page into a format a computer can use.

Screen Saver
A moving picture or pattern that appears on the screen when a computer is not used for a period of time.

SCSI
Small Computer System Interface. A fast and flexible, although expensive, way of connecting hard drives and other devices to a computer.

Serial Port
A type of socket at the back of a computer where you plug in a mouse, modem or scanner. It has either 9 or 25 pins.

Server
A computer that stores the information of every computer connected to a client/server network.

GLOSSARY

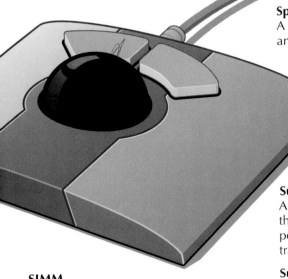

SIMM
Single In-Line Memory Module. A circuit board inside a computer that holds memory chips.

Software
A set of electronic instructions that tell a computer what to do. It lets you accomplish tasks, such as writing letters or playing games.

Sound Card
A circuit board that improves the sound quality of a computer. Also called a sound board or audio card.

Spooler
A program in a computer that stores the information you selected to print. It lets you continue using a computer without waiting for a document to finish printing.

Spreadsheet
A program used to manage, analyze and present financial information.

SRAM
Static Random Access Memory. The most expensive type of memory. It works at very high speeds to improve the performance of a computer.

Subnotebook
A type of portable computer that weighs between two and six pounds. It is ideal for frequent travelers.

Suite
A collection of programs by one manufacturer in a single package.

Surge
A fluctuation in power that can occur during a storm or when power returns after a power failure.

Surge Protector
A device that protects a computer from damage due to fluctuations in power, called surges.

T

Table
1. A feature in a word processor used to organize information into rows and columns. 2. A collection of information in a database about a particular subject.

Tape Drive
A device that lets you copy the information stored on a computer to tape cartridges. Also called a tape backup unit.

Thermal-Wax Color Printer
A type of printer that produces sharp, rich, non-smearing, color images. It is ideal for prepress work and for producing color overhead transparencies.

Token-Ring
A way of exchanging information between computers on a network. A computer attaches information to an electronic token, which passes around the network until it reaches its destination.

Tower Case
A tall, narrow computer case that usually sits on the floor.

Trackball
An upside-down mouse that remains stationary. It controls the position of the mouse pointer on the screen.

Typeface
The design of characters. Some examples are `Courier`, **Helvetica** and Times New Roman.

Type Size
The size of characters, measured in points. There are approximately 72 points in one inch.

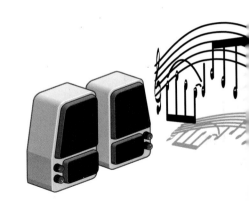

U

Undo
A feature in many programs that cancels the last change you made.

Uninterruptible Power Supply (UPS)
A device that protects a computer from damage due to power loss or fluctuations in power.

V

Video Adapter
A circuit board inside a computer that controls the images displayed on a screen.

Virus
A program that disrupts the normal operation of a computer. For example, it can display annoying messages on a screen or destroy information on a hard drive.

VL-Bus
A high-speed type of bus that is primarily used to send information to a monitor. It is used in 486 computers.

VRAM
Video Random Access Memory. A high-speed type of memory that temporarily stores information to be displayed on the screen.

W

Wavetable Synthesis
One way that a sound card can produce sound. It produces rich, realistic sound by using actual recordings of musical instruments.

Wide Area Network (WAN)
A network that connects computers across a large geographic area, such as a city or country.

Window
A rectangle on a screen that displays information.

Windows
A graphics-based program that controls the overall activity of a computer.

Word Processor
A program with editing and formatting features for producing documents.

Word Wrapping
A feature in a word processor that automatically moves words to the next line as you type.

Z

ZIF Socket
Zero Insertion Force socket. A type of socket that makes it easy to remove and replace a chip in a computer.

INDEX

INDEX

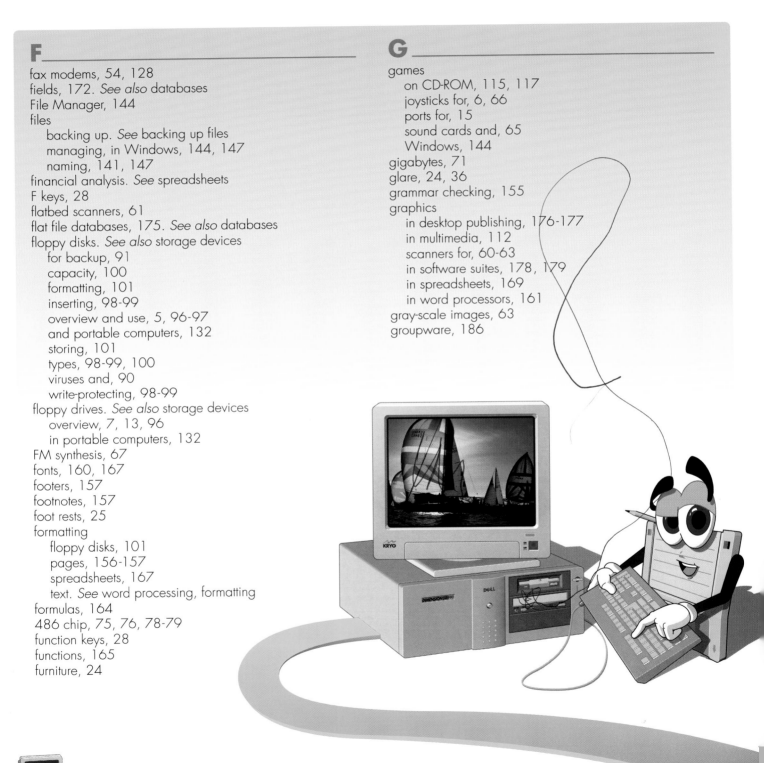

INDEX

INDEX